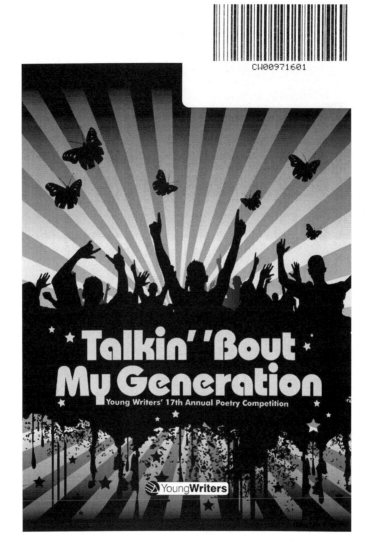

Young Writers' 17th Annual Poetry Competition

YoungWriters

Staffordshire
Edited by Annabel Cook

 Young**Writers**

First published in Great Britain in 2008 by:
Young Writers
Remus House
Coltsfoot Drive
Peterborough
PE2 9JX
Telephone: 01733 890066
Website: www.youngwriters.co.uk

SB ISBN 978-1 84431 487 4

Foreword

This year, the Young Writers' *Talkin' 'Bout My Generation* competition proudly presents a showcase of the best poetic talent selected from thousands of up-and-coming writers nationwide.

Young Writers was established in 1991 to promote the reading and writing of poetry within schools and to the young of today. Our books nurture and inspire confidence in the ability of young writers and provide a snapshot of poems written in schools and at home by budding poets of the future.

The thought, effort, imagination and hard work put into each poem impressed us all and the task of selecting poems was a difficult but nevertheless enjoyable experience.

We hope you are as pleased as we are with the final selection and that you and your family continue to be entertained with *Talkin' 'Bout My Generation Staffordshire* for many years to come.

Contents

Endon High School

Lucy Neat (13)	1
Emily Williamson (14)	2
Abigail Sutton (14)	4
Emily Cartlidge (14)	5

Painsley Catholic College

Ben Starkey (11)	5
Chris Gibson (11)	6
Jacob Mills (11)	6
Joe Bird (11)	7
Saim Khaliq (14)	8
Rach Ottley (15)	9
Elizabeth Spooner (11)	10
Bartosz Wozniak (13)	11
Emma-Jane Malkin (12)	12
Emma Robinson (11)	12
Tyler Moore (12)	13
Emily Saxon (11)	13
Shannon Alkins (11)	14
Ben Staton (11)	14
Sophie Buckley (11)	15
Harry Hartley (12)	15
Olivia Smith (11)	16
Zach Brassington (11)	16
Alexander Harvey (11)	17
Joe Emery (11)	17
Luke Morgan (11)	18
Jonathan Whitehurst (12)	18
Gavin Oliver (11)	19
Thomas Mulley (11)	19
Andrew Humphreys (15)	20
Vanessa Stevenson (12)	20
Daniel Snow (12)	21
Josh Hughes-Johnson (12)	21
Angela Coleclough (15)	22
Harry Smith (12)	22
Sam Phillips (12)	23
Laura Slaney (12)	23

Hollie Morrison (12)	24
Daniel Toon (11)	24
Charlotte Leyland (13)	25
Holly Jones (12)	25
Rebecca Wright (13)	26
William Jones (12)	27
Hannah Stanway (12)	28
Lucinda Wilks (12)	28
Natalie Torr (12)	29
Jakob Pickthorne (11)	29
Kimberley Ball (12)	30
Oliver Good (11)	30
Mark Fallows (11)	31
Beth Foster (13)	31
Molly Boughey (12)	32
Hannah Cooper (13)	32
Elizabeth Kaine (12)	33
Laura Woodroffe (12)	33
Christopher Hughes (11)	34
Daniel Allen (13)	34
Josh Jones (13)	35
Holly O'Rourke (11)	35
Bromwyn Goodwin (11)	36
Adam Khalifa (12)	36
Gabriella Cordall (12)	37
Jessica Cooper (13)	37
Daniel Boot (12)	38
Adam Cordall (12)	39
Sarah Dudley (13)	39
Kate Harding (12)	40
Luisa Thorley (11)	40
Oliver Stott (11)	41
Mollie Smith (11)	41
Emily Scarlett (12)	42
Lee Minor (11)	42
Nicola Campbell (11)	43
Amy Hurst (11)	43
Robert Morris (13)	44
Anna Kilgannon (11)	45
Ellis Maguire (13)	46
Chloe Moore (11)	47
Madalaine Forrester (11)	48

Mark Finney (11)	48
Joseph Unyolo (13)	49
Aaron Booth (11)	49
Siobhan Hunt (13)	50
Karsen Poon (11)	50
Ryan Molloy (13)	51
Gabriella Licata (11)	51
Naomi Tyers (13)	52
Martha Sowter (13)	53
Emily Campbell (13)	54
Annabel Emery (13)	55
Izaak Bailey (13)	56
Emily Hulme (13)	57
Seb Morrell (13)	58
Stephen Phillips (11)	58
Daniel Davis (13)	59
Rebecca O'Connor (11)	59
Rhiannon Gibson (13)	60
Megan Prins (11)	60
Rachelle Cooper (11)	61
Jack Degg (11)	61
Callum Bradbury (11)	62
Tam Bowyer (11)	62
Georgina Bailey (11)	63
Leah Machin (11)	63
Kieren O'Leary (11)	64
Rachel Sollitt (11)	64
Nicholas Perkin (11)	65
Richard Williams (11)	65
Kieran Carnwell (11)	66
Alice Pattinson (11)	67
Rebecca Mountford (12)	68
Georgia Thorley (11)	69
Kacper Wozniak (11)	70
Thomas Baskeyfield (11)	71
Callum Pegg (11)	71
Danni McCormack (11)	72
Charlie Loughran (11)	72
Amy McKenna (11)	73
Sam Tyers (11)	73
Liam Kelly (12)	74
Zoe Hurst (13)	74

Lizzie Casey (11)	75
James Smith (11)	75
Yasmin Hurst (11)	76
Bradley Moult (11)	76
Sean Hullah (11)	77
Joanna Beard (11)	77
Eleanor Smith (12)	78
Rachel Roberts	79
Rhianne Sutton (11)	80
Tom Plant (11)	80
Daniel Capper (11)	81
Connor Hardisty (12) & Alex Hardisty (13)	81
Samuel Stephens (11)	82
Jessica Miller (12)	82
Adam Peaty (12)	83
Bradley Finney (11)	83
Charlotte Goldstraw (11)	84
Zoë Darbyshire (13)	84
Alex Green (11)	85
Stephen Sammons (12)	85
Charlotte Hubble (11)	86
James O'Connor (11)	86
Bethany Pearson (12)	87
Jacob Lovatt (12)	87
Olivia Edge (12)	88
Callum Downie (12)	88
Joseph Cooper (12)	89
Aaron Eyre (11)	89
Matt Spooner (13)	90
India Cotton (12)	91
Sally-Ann Dunn (12)	92
Ashleigh Humphrey (12)	93
Sullivan Edwards (11)	94
Christopher Bullock (12)	94
Bethany Godwin (13)	95
Robin Khadjenouri (14)	95
Matthew Priddey (14)	96
Lucinda Caton-Tanner (13)	96
Jack Pearson (13)	97
Sophie Bullock (13)	97
Hazel Cross (13)	98
Courtney Smith (14)	98

Gabrielle Byrne (12)	99
Jacob Perks (13)	99
Jack Bourne (13)	100
Lucy Chadwick (12)	100
Lucy Goodwin (12)	101
Philippa Oakden (13)	101
Jessica Greensmith (12)	102
Isobel Alkins (12)	102
Georgia Bennett (12)	103
Connor Forrester (12)	103
Hannah Griffin (12)	104
Kieran Barron (12)	104
Stacey Osborne (12)	105

Ryecroft CE Middle School

Calum Stratton (12)	105
Dan Lear (12)	106
Jack Martin (11)	106
Emma Addison (11)	107
Reuben Wilson (11)	107
Tristan Marsh (12)	108
Kelly Walker (11)	108
Jasmin Martin (11)	109
Fern Adams (12)	109
Sophie Robotham (11)	110
Georgina Stokes (12)	111
Ben Clowes (11)	112
Rebecca Ward (11)	112
Harley Bussey (11)	113
Polly Clowes (11)	113
Emily Heathcote (11)	114
Aaron Stones (11)	114
Anthony Lane (11)	115
Kristie Beddoes (11)	115
Harriet Brodie (11)	116
Martha Baker (11)	116
William Heathcote (11)	117
Declan Lander (12)	117
Joe Cliffe (11)	118

St Dominic's School, Brewood

Eliza Ollerenshaw (12)	118
Laura Tarbuck (14)	119
Hollie Read (11)	119
Charlotte Davies (11)	120
Maneshia Johal (11)	120
Molly Hyson (12)	121
Jordana O'Reilly (12)	121
Hannah Cox (11)	122
Elizabeth Butler (12)	122
Demie Allport (13)	123
Annabel Randev (13)	123
Hannah Smith (13)	124
Abigail Watkins (12)	125
Katherine Rigg (11)	125
Rachel Hollingsworth (14)	126
Charlotte Jones (11)	126
Henrietta Painter (13)	127
Katie Woods (13)	127
Charlotte Grainger (12)	128
Georgina Wood (12)	128
Hannah Bowen (12)	129
Salma Nadim (12)	129
Jessica Mackriel (12)	130
Aoife Richardson (12)	131
Lydia Dyer (12)	132
Chloë Sharifi (12)	132
Emily Loveitt (11)	133
Poppy Benkwitz (12)	133
Ellie Durnall (14)	134
Hannah Sefton (13)	134

St Thomas More Catholic College, Stoke-on-Trent

Philip Hallworth (12)	135
Ann Johnson (12)	135
Susannah Owen (12)	136
Jack Twigg (12)	136
Catherine Hawley (12)	137
Holly Marie Dunn (11)	137
Flora Byatt (12)	138
Hannah Rickard (11)	138

Keira Taylor (12)	139
Matthew Gordon (12)	139
Savannah Fradley (12)	140
Helena Wegierak (12)	140
Junaid Ishfaq (11)	141
Kayleigh Cooper (11)	141
Luke Critchlow (12)	142
Lauren West (13)	142
Danny Boulton (11)	143
Bethany Baskeyfield (11)	143
Luke Boulton (13)	144
Amy Thomas (12)	144
William Plant (11)	145
Lucy Niemczyk (12)	145
Lauren Jade Ashton (12)	146
Connel Brownsword (11)	146
Chloe Jane Lawton (11)	147
Lauren Tomkinson (11)	147
Cicely Lane (11)	148
Thomas Johnson (12)	148
Stephanie Hughes (13)	149
Jessica Bould (11)	149
Holly Rutter (12)	150
Chloe-Ann Lythgoe (12)	150
Ellise Nicholls (11)	151
Hayley Plant (11)	151
Georgia Birch (11)	152
Andrew Cash (11)	152
Connor Wood (11)	153
Adam Stanway (12)	153
Robert Sangwa (11)	154
Demi Robinshaw (11)	155
Hannah Gibson (11)	156
Mia Kimberley (11)	156
Benjamin Gibson (11)	157
Lydia Derbyshire (11)	157
Jessica Elikowski (12)	158
Olivia Tatler (11)	158
Aimee Birks (12)	159
Charlotte Melia (12)	159
Taylor Simms (11)	160
Samantha Clarke (12)	160

Jake Anthony (11)	161
Daniel Kane (12)	161
Ben Diliberto (11)	162
Joelle Littlejohn (12)	162
Kelly Bryan (11)	163
Jake Smith (11)	163
Ryan Fulcher (11)	164
Jonathan James Toft (11)	164
Ruby Davies (11)	165
Nathalie Woolliscroft (11)	165

Sir Graham Balfour School

Ashleigh Davies (12)	166
James Hewitt (12)	167
Harry Farmer (12)	168
Ellie Ralph (12)	168
Annabel Ryell (13)	169
Sam Paterson (12)	169
Amy Howard (13)	170
Daniella Richards (12)	170
Andrew Peatfield (12)	171
Amy-Rose Bayliffe	171
Suzanne Butters (12)	172
Sam Alexander (12)	172
Hazel Jackson (12)	173
Olivia Graham (12)	173
Carissa Alderman (13)	174
Macauley Blencowe (13)	174
John Handley (12)	175
Kyle Cooper (12)	175
Helen Rogers (12)	176

Two Rivers Sixth Form

Lee Rudd (17)	176
Dan Berry (16)	177
Shane Moore (16)	177
Ann-Marie Robbins (17)	178
Claire Griffiths (17)	179
Nicole Sayce (16)	180

The Poems

Cliques

Today's so very different;
From yesterday and the past.
All I want to know is,
How long will it last?

Everyone is separated,
Into different cliques.
There's the 'populars', the 'fashionables',
The 'emos' and 'the geeks'.

You don't even get to choose,
Where you want to be.
Peers take one look at you,
Take you for what they see.

If you are with 'the geeks',
Sometimes it feels so bad;
No one really gets to know you,
It makes you feel so mad.

Then there is the 'emos';
They're stereotyped too.
Just because they're a little different,
Doesn't mean they aren't like you.

Next there are the 'populars'.
What could go wrong there?
They just want attention,
Want people to stand and stare.

Everything is all so wrong;
It shouldn't be this way,
Everyone should be all together,
And everyone should have a say.

Lucy Neat (13)
Endon High School

Teacher Vs Pupil

'You're greedy and selfish'
They don't mind to call
'Stand up, sit down
Don't slouch, look tall.'

'Greedy and selfish
Is that what you think
What about when I was thirsty
But you refused to share your drink.'

'Well that was different
And never you mind
In my day, with this backchat
You'd have a smacked behind.

Back in my day,
Was different back then,
From you it's all I hear
Now hand me your pen.'

'I believe the word's please
And you don't need a pen
Stop always wanting things
Use your manners and come back then.'

'I do use my manners
And what's it to you
And even when you have things
You still want more new.'

'You're disrespectful,
You don't have care,
I suppose it's your upbringing,
That you're only bothered
About your hair.'

'Well I can be silly
But I can be good
I bet you were like me
In your childhood.'

'Well we used to play football
And meet people face to face
But you rely on that Internet
It's the same with any race.'

'Stop going on at me
Like your dad did to you
My generation has its problems
Like yours did too.'

'I suppose I could agree
But you're lucky, you don't realise
You have more options, open up your eyes.'

'Yes you're right, but with options
There comes pressure
We're pushed to grow up with tests
It's an unnecessary measure.'

'Hmm I never thought of that,
I guess we're both right,
It was so long ago,
I guess I lost sight.'

Emily Williamson (14)
Endon High School

Teenage Differences

She walks down the road
In her band T-shirt and her dirty black Converse
She really doesn't think she has a purpose
She feels like she's on her own.

He walks down the road
In his designer jacket and his brand new Reeboks
Thank God he's wearing jeans not trackie bottoms tucked in socks
Everyone knows who he is.

They don't acknowledge each other
They really don't think it's worth the bother
They have feelings inside
There ain't no point tryin' to hide.

Emo is what they call her she's a no go zone
His mates shout abuse over the road
Her mates scream over the wrapping overload
They just want to be left alone.

They don't acknowledge each other
They really don't think it's worth the bother
They have feelings inside
There ain't no point tryin' to hide.

Finally they start emailing each other
Maybe kids could learn to live together

Then they could have a happily ever after.

Abigail Sutton (14)
Endon High School

My Love Generation

A certain someone can take your heart forever
To glance and fall head over heels
Made for each other
So what should stop but time.

But there's a barrier between the two
A shadow overcast upon
As they search and move forward
Minds think of each other.

Breaking hearts and bleeding songs
If only there was no one to interfere
Neither can let go of what should belong
Is it time to move on?

Regardless of surrounding interruptions
Found and loved again
But what should come in the way
If both would die for each other.

Why was half the heart cold?
Why were tears occurring?
Blood trickling
Emotions dead.

Am I good enough for you now?

Emily Cartlidge (14)
Endon High School

My Family

My family is quite small
They drive me up the wall
There's one girl in my family that is my mother
But then comes my brother
My dad runs around
But he does get a crowd.

Ben Starkey (11)
Painsley Catholic College

Talkin' 'Bout My Generation

T alkin' 'bout my generation,
A nd how we live our lives today.
L ookin' at the things around me
K nowing how computers work.
I nto PS2s and iPods
N ever used to be this way.

B eing with your mates at weekend
O r family and pets, is so relaxing before
U phill struggles like school work and
T ests, in which you hope to do well in all of the time.

M aybe next time I'll be top of the class.
Y esterday I forgot to revise!

G iving and receiving presents,
E ating cake and mince pies is such a
N ice sensation at Christmas time, but
E very time I take a bite, I
R eally start to think,
A bout all of the people in the world,
T hat don't have the money for food or drink.
I f there were any chance in my life to go
O ver there and help those poor people
N ow would be the best time - this is my generation.

Chris Gibson (11)
Painsley Catholic College

The Shark

S hooting through the sea like an arrow
H unting prey for its babies
A ttacking prey for itself
R ampaging shark eating anything in its sight
K illers of the ocean.

Jacob Mills (11)
Painsley Catholic College

A Cat

Here I am, on the window sill
Looking outside, staying so still,
My master comes home, in his car
I look at him and think *what a star!*

I go outside to go and greet him
On his face, there is a happy grin,
He'll think that I'm in a good mood,
When all I only want is food!

I let him stroke me and call me 'Puss'
He seems to think I like the fuss,
All I want is for him to leave me alone
'Cause all I want is his nice comfortable home!

I go inside and then I see
A great big portion of food for me,
I look at the bowl on the floor
If I eat this now will I have some more?

When my master comes and calls
'Pussy!'
I wonder why is he so fussy?
I run to him and sit on his lap
And then I have a very long nap.

It's a hard life being a cat,
Why doesn't anyone
Understand that!

Joe Bird (11)
Painsley Catholic College

Through The Eyes Of Me

I can't see the colours of the day,
I can't hear the sweet singing of the birds.
I can't speak to the animals around me,
I can't do anything.

I haven't got a name or a nationality,
I have no family or any friends.
I have no home, shelter or any rights,
I'm the loneliest person on Earth.

I've never seen myself before,
I don't know what colour I am.
My hands are my eyes my ears and my mouth,
I can only touch and feel but sometimes I wish I couldn't
                                        do those either.

I have no shoulder to rest my head on,
I have no hand to hold when I'm in need.
I have no one who I can embrace when I cry,
I have no one who I can call as my own.

Everyone feels sorry for me,
But they can't feel any irritation or grief.
I despise living in this world where pain is my only friend,
I search for salvation and comfort every single day.

Sometimes I wish I could depart this life,
Anything would be better than this.
I wish I had senses that would work,
But more I wish I was a normal person, I crave for that life.

I live between life and death,
Everyday is full of sorrow, hardship and agony for me.
Every moment I ask myself who I am,
Nobody knows how I feel, except for me.

Saim Khaliq (14)
Painsley Catholic College

The Journey

The journey of life begun
That fateful day I was born
My eyes opened up blissfully to the sun
My soul, heart and brain emerged as one
Behold my journey had begun!

This little child in time has grown
Yes! Time has flown, time has flown
A lot has been learnt on my very own.

Life has been a mystifying journey
With every up and down
With tears and laughter
With hate and love
With stupidity and wisdom
With enemies and friends
But even in my journey of frustration
I have found a means of celebration
In my toilsome exploration to my fateful destination.

Tick-tock the clock goes on
Minute by minute then hourly
Month my month then yearly
Tick-tock and in my journey
I have searched, questioned and answered
Whilst walking painfully along many paths
Sometimes requesting protection
Seeking from above immunisation
When hit by obstacles in locations.

But I am still on this journey
Shaking hands with the sad and merry
My passion for life which was once raw
Is now confined within the Almighty's law
For life's journey itself never ends
Once you have reached the end of each road
Uplifting off your entire cloggy load
Be it in a hot summer or a winter's cold
Behold! A new journey will unfold.

Rach Ottley (15)
Painsley Catholic College

A Friend Indeed

She treats people like royalty
She gets treated like the Queen.
Everyone loves her smiley face,
Her teeth, a shiny white gleam.
She's always been the popular one,
But behind her white smile,
I think she's unhappy, she's quit school
I haven't seen her in a while.
Last time we saw,
Anything of her face
She was wearing what she always wore,
In our little place.
She told me something awful had happened
Between her mum and dad
Although she was really being brave I could tell that she was sad
With hot chocolate and marshmallows
I tried to cheer her up
Her hands were very cold
And clasped around the cup.
She's locked herself away
She doesn't even answer her phone
I really wanted to help her
But she wants to be alone.

A friend I had
A friend in need
A friend I miss
Huh, a friend indeed.

Elizabeth Spooner (11)
Painsley Catholic College

Through The Eyes Of A Lego Man

I am a handsome Lego man
Everyone calls me Fabulous Dan.
Even though, my brain is plastic,
It does not stop me from being fantastic!

Sometimes I lay in the box, all day long,
Some days, I fight a Lego King Kong.
Often I get tortured by my owner's sister,
Next day, I am fixed, by my magic master.

Today, my owner is building me a huge house,
However to him, it is only the size of a small mouse.
It is going to have all the latest goods,
And a pair of brand new football studs.

He also built me a brand new modern car,
At night, I will try to go to the bar.
I hope tomorrow, he will fix my friend,
The one that is so ill, he can't even bend.

My owner promised me, he will build a pool,
So when hot days come, my body can cool.
I am going to have a party, invite all my mates,
I will be very proudly welcoming them at the gates.

Overall, I have to say - my life is interesting,
Quite often, I just lie there in my bed resting.
Seeing through my window, the difficult life of human,
I honestly am happy, that I am a plastic Lego man.

Bartosz Wozniak (13)
Painsley Catholic College

Deals On Wheels

I breezed along the pavement,
Amongst the passing crowd.
The whispers they got louder,
Of the people standing there.

They looked at me with pity,
Which angered me so much.
As all these able people,
Could be so out of touch.

The end of the street came near,
The council are to blame.
They hadn't dropped the kerb,
And the potholes were the same.

I struggled up the hills,
But not going down.
My wheelchair brakes had failed,
And I sailed down like a clown.

My arms they were waving,
Would I ever be the same?
No one tried to stop me,
No win, no fee. Let's claim!

Emma-Jane Malkin (12)
Painsley Catholic College

From The Eyes Of A Baby

You try to get their attention but they just smile.
So you pretend to sleep and then wait a while.
Then you start to scream and shout.
'Pick me up! Let me out!'
They slowly reach down to pick you up.
'Come on! Hurry up!'
'Don't you understand? I want something to eat!'
'I can't stand on my own two feet!'
They're so annoying! Pulling lots of funny faces.
Don't they realise it's very babyish!

Emma Robinson (11)
Painsley Catholic College

My Poem

I'm a celebrity
I'm famous, I'm a star
I'm popular and funny
I'm the best by far.

I love to sing
I love to dance
I'm simply the best
Just give me a chance.

Let me show you
Just what I can do
I'll sing you a song
Or even two.

If you like them
Sing along with me
And then maybe
I'll sing you three.

Clap your hands to the music
Get up and dance on your feet
There's no need to stay
Sat in your seat.

Tyler Moore (12)
Painsley Catholic College

My Grandma

Peggy Alcock's ever so slim,
She wears glasses because her eyes are dim,
She comes on a Sunday after we've had lunch,
And when she's there we're such a bunch,
Laughing and joking she makes some fun,
And when we've had tea,
She'll go home and sit in the sun.

Emily Saxon (11)
Painsley Catholic College

My Family And Friends

There's my mum
There's my dad,
There's my nan, Gran
My grandad too,
There's my aunties,
And my uncles,
My sisters and my brothers,
I've got cousins too,
I've got friends
Who are kind,
A best friend too
And guess what
I'm a generation too.

Shannon Alkins (11)
Painsley Catholic College

The Blind Man

I woke up one morning, blind,
I looked in front and behind,
I felt for the phone then I screamed
And I groaned and never saw the light again.
In case you don't know, my name's Tim
And my brother's called Jim,
And we are both poor
And I think what more?
That morning when I found the phone,
I phoned my nana, Joan,
She phoned my niece
And wasn't in one piece
When she found out I was blind.

Ben Staton (11)
Painsley Catholic College

A Helping Hand

I live in a world of computers,
A world of plasma screens and mp3s.

Microwave dinners that go ping when they are done,
Not half as much fun as baking with Mum.

It seems to me, in spite of technology,
I will always need someone to love,
And God's help from above.

A strong arm around me,
From when I was a baby,

Showing me the way,
We should live every day.

Sophie Buckley (11)
Painsley Catholic College

The Bullying

Bullies I hate them so,
Every day they get me down,
Every day I wish they'd go
The playground is a battlefield,
They threaten me every day
So I never tell, make a sound, and pretend I
Have nothing to say,
Grazes, I say I feel,
Bruises, cuts and slit lips,
I ignore them and say nothing, nothing at all;
Because I know I'd end up in Hell,
I choose never to tell.

Harry Hartley (12)
Painsley Catholic College

My Generation

My generation starts with me.
I am the oldest child in the family,
I am the first to have run in the sun
I am the one who is first to have fun.

I'm lucky to be born in the time that I am
I have plenty to eat and eat all that I can
There is electricity, phones and TV
Oh how lucky can I be.

My granny Kit had a toilet outside
Where spiders and slugs would often hide
A pantry to house all the food they would eat
Not a cooling fridge to keep things neat.

I'm sure I would manage if I had to cope
With living with them in grime and smoke
I hope there are changes and an environmental revelation
So that we can pass on good things to the next generation.

Olivia Smith (11)
Painsley Catholic College

Football

This is such a beautiful game, you can kick it,
Bounce it and throw it with all your might.
You need control, balance and skill to play it.
There are teams which play this game all of them love it too.
So what is this game? Football's the name.
Everyone can see it, playing it and feeling it.
It can make your life wonderful there are players which play
this game,
Such as Steven Gerrard, Cristiano Ronaldo and lots more . . .
So this game is thought as part of life.

Zach Brassington (11)
Painsley Catholic College

Talkin' 'Bout My Generation

My generation is really cool
We enjoy playing pool
My PSP is really fun
We like to play it in the sun.

Sometimes I ride on my bike
But when we get a puncture we have to hike
We like to have some tasty food
Especially when we are in a good mood.

Weekends are best with pocket money cash
To the sweet shop we love to dash
Weekends are a good time for my leisure
Watching 'The Simpsons' is a pleasure.

Alexander Harvey (11)
Painsley Catholic College

The Awful Adults!

Every adult has something against teens,
They think we're lean, mean vandalising machines,
They think we're loose cannons ready to
Explode and reckless on the roads.
They were just like us once with all the new trends
But now it seems a crime to just hang with your friends.
Why do you think we're always breaking the law,
Is it 'cause we're having fun that you can't take anymore?
So I say why, why all the fuss 'cause
Remember you were just like us.

Joe Emery (11)
Painsley Catholic College

My Generation

It seems like yesterday that my dad was talking
To his grandad that's how fast time goes in these days
And time will tell and from one generation to another.
People come and people go, that's how fast generations move on.

I guess it is a well-known fact that every generation thinks
Theirs is a better than the one before
We are always hearing people say 'in my days' and 'in
                                          my generation',
This would not happen or we would not do that,
But this is just how generations progress.

Luke Morgan (11)
Painsley Catholic College

Animals

Dogs cats, birds and hamsters are treated so fairly nowadays,
But before that every animal was being tortured and killed
And all of the animals were dying.
We lost a lot of species, but thankfully we saved a lot too.

Dogs, cats, birds and hamsters are not going to be threatened
                                                    anymore,
So let's keep nature safe so nothing will kill them, especially bears
                                                    and gorillas.

Jonathan Whitehurst (12)
Painsley Catholic College

My Generation

We are the kids of 2008,
We like to hang out with our mates.

We play on Xbox or PS2
And support Chelsea or Man U.

If it's information that we need,
The World Wide Web will give it to us at speed.

Our planet is not very clean,
So we've been told that we have to go green.

Our generation will have a lot to do,
To make sure that the world is always here for me and you!

Gavin Oliver (11)
Painsley Catholic College

My Generation!

As we walk down the road what do we see?
Hoodie tops, trackie tops, it's all the same to me.
No individuality, it's all copy, copy me.

Not many manners, not much for us to see
Old people get scared of the crowds they see.
Come on you young ones see the life I see
Make this place a better one for you and for me.

Thomas Mulley (11)
Painsley Catholic College

The Age Of The King

In the far future mankind is run by one man, King George 12th,
He is the king of mankind, a race which is doomed to die.
The galaxy spanning empire is a place of murder and high treason
And slaughter in the name of the High King.

Sacrifices are made daily in their millions to support and give the king
Power of the gods in the heavens, the secret order of the inquisition
Enforce that these daily sacrifices are carried out.

A single man is one in untold billions on over a million planets
Which span the lathias mothenium, the former Milky Way,
The empire is ran from Holy Terra formerly known as Earth.

This is an age of demise and Regicides wishing to take the throne,
This is an age of war!

Andrew Humphreys (15)
Painsley Catholic College

Good Samaritan

Our world today, holds nothing but pain,
There's so many poor people who just stand in the rain,
No food to eat or home to go,
No TV to watch or water to flow,
They stand all alone, but it starts to get dark,
So they get ready for another sleep on the bench in the park,
Sleeping so cold, no blanket to keep them warm,
They never let it show, but inside they are torn,
Our world today, is no place to live,
So be a good Samaritan, and give all you can give.

Vanessa Stevenson (12)
Painsley Catholic College

Dan's Poem

Here I am at my desk, thinking about my past,
I am 12 years old and can't believe how it's gone so fast.
I was 2 years old as good as gold.
Nothing could go wrong,
Yeah right that's until a sister came along.
We have good times, we've had bad times,
Times we ran our luck,
I've even been accused of constantly winding her up!
As we grow up there are lots of things that are good and bad,
Even when my dad starts, 'When I was a lad!'
One thing for sure as I grow up the world's getting greener,
You can't eat this, you can't do that!
It's also getting meaner.
When I leave school and get a job, even buy my own place,
Maybe by then you never know it could be in outer space!

Daniel Snow (12)
Painsley Catholic College

The 60s Generation

My dad was born in '69
My mum was born in '68
They were too late to see these famous singing groups
Rolling Stones, The Beatles and The Who
But they weren't too late to see the World Cup
And hear about the man on the moon.
Also the most tragic in the 60s
Assassinations of JFK and MLK
And the worst the Vietnam War.

Josh Hughes-Johnson (12)
Painsley Catholic College

Meaning Of Life

The meaning of life,
Be careful what you wish for,
Think bad,
Feel bad,
Get bad.
With a flip of a coin,
Feel good,
Get good.

Be thankful for what you have got,
And you will get more.

Picture your hands,
Holding something special,
And you will receive.

Angela Coleclough (15)
Painsley Catholic College

My Generation

G enerations happen
E very day
N o one knows how it
E nds
R oaming
A round
T ime flies by
I n a minute, one gets
O lder, then all of a sudden there is a
N ew generation.

Harry Smith (12)
Painsley Catholic College

Smudge

My dog is called Smudge.
She eats lots of fudge.
When I say, come here;
She will disappear.
When she goes out to play
She likes to jump in the hay.
She chews on Mum's cardigan
And roots on her garden.
Then Mum gets cross,
Smudge knows she is the boss.
The milkman is her mate,
She hopes he won't be late
Because when he comes
There are always biscuits for her to eat.

Sam Phillips (12)
Painsley Catholic College

Generation

G randad's passing family traditions on
E ating food made with Nana's secret recipes
N ever telling those well-kept family secrets
E ach passed down from family members
R unning around during family parties
A mazed by the food on offer
T ime for a kickabout with Dad
I love times like this
O ne of many more to come
N ever-ending generations.

Laura Slaney (12)
Painsley Catholic College

Katie's Fairy Tale

Jordan, Katie, playgirl, princess, party girl, mother, tabloid princess,
All of these things,
But like any girl, my biggest dream is a fairytale wedding
A wedding like you've never seen.

My prince was from the jungle and
The nation watched as we fell in love and
Bickered a lot. The press was shocked
When he asked me to be his mysterious girl,
And said, I make you mine.

A Cinderella dress with ten thousand pink crystals,
Diamonds, tiara, glitz and glamour
I wanted this day to last forever
But the best thing of all
My Prince Charming shining and dressed in white
He took my hand and made me his wife.

The press mocked and said it was too much,
Tacky and over the top.
But I am richer then you can imagine in every way,
A husband, a family, and wealth beyond your wildest dreams.
Never one to mince my words, say what you like
This is my answer, so laugh if you like.

Hollie Morrison (12)
Painsley Catholic College

Life

Life is a fire that burns as an ember then starts to burn as
a mighty fire,
Then it lights another fire but the first fire burns out
Leaving tiny embers which each become mighty fires too
Just like human life each one its own generation.

Daniel Toon (11)
Painsley Catholic College

That's Not The Real Me!

Pictures, plastered all over the front pages,
Mistakes made from the night before,
I didn't really mean it, I can't remember it all!
But that's not the real me!

Really, I'm quite calm and serene,
Who keeps myself to myself,
What's written in the newspapers, is a lie!
That isn't the real me!

Internet forums and blogs with my name all over it,
What's written inside them is wrong.
Paparazzi cameras flashing in my eyes,
Everyone trying to get a picture of me, not looking my best!
But who cares - not me!

My millionaire status, is what makes me known to everyone,
But what you see, is what you get with me,
And never judge a book by its cover,
In reality, I'm a totally different person.

Just get to know me, and you will see,
What person I really am inside,
I'm really a friendly person with a heart of gold,
I am really just misunderstood!

Charlotte Leyland (13)
Painsley Catholic College

My Little Cousin

I have a little cousin Max Thomas is his name.

He goes to Socatots to learn the football game.

He runs and jumps, kicks and throws and also runs around
On his tiny little toes.

He plays the game and has such fun and then is allowed to play
with his mum.

Holly Jones (12)
Painsley Catholic College

Through The Eyes Of A Young Monkey

Each day I swing from vine to vine,
Then I look for food at about quarter-past nine.
I usually have 50 nuts and 10 bananas.
Then I go along and visit my nana's.
She lives up in the tallest tree,
On my way up I pass the nest of the queen bee!
My nana has a monkey nut,
And she has a cup of tea then down it's put.
Then we say 'oo oo ah ah',
When it's time for me to go home,
I always have a little roam.
I often pass some of my friends,
The talking always extends,
To the point where I see my mum and dad looking for me,
When they do they jump with glee!
They always say 'Too much talking'
Then I say 'I know I should have been walking'
They forgive me and off I go,
To find out something I ought to know.
That something is how to flip,
But then I lose my grip.
I put my hands down and do the things I most wanted,
When I told my friends I got taunted.

Rebecca Wright (13)
Painsley Catholic College

Through The Eyes Of A River

I start in the sky a little strange I know
Falling to the ground is where I will go
Starting on a hillside, as a little stream
Flowing and flowing I start to gleam
As I reach the bottom of the hill
The whole river basin is what I fill
I'm a raging torrent heading for the sea
All of a sudden there is something diverting me.

The water works I think is where I am going
What's going to happen there I'm not knowing
As I head in they clean and clean
Now I know I really gleam
I go through a pipe and another
I'm feeling dizzy now, 'Oh bother'
Through a pipe I'm nearly at the end
Soon very soon round one more bend!

I burst out of the pipe and into a glass
Gulp, gulp, gulp, out of that pipe at last
Hang on someone is drinking me from a glass
I'm hitting the sides of the new pipes bash!
Flowing down then all of a sudden splash
Swilling round now a flush and a crash
I keep going on through the water works all bashed
Flowing down the river and into the sea (at last!)

William Jones (12)
Painsley Catholic College

Lonely Little School Girl

Lonely is that little girl who sits at school all day,
Once waiting for some friends so she too, could go and play.
No one makes the effort to smile or simple chat,
Lonely little school girl will not even whisper back.
Everyone ignores her,
You'll not even notice she's there,
Like a piece of furniture,
It's almost as if she's not there.
Truth be known she (I) died last week,
Time flies by when you go without a squeak.
Lonely little school girl dragged into a car,
Everybody could see what was happening from afar.
Ghostly little school girl,
I'm talking now as you can see,
Rarely, yes I know.
Lonely little school girl, who is she?

Hannah Stanway (12)
Painsley Catholic College

Through The Eyes Of . . . An Indie Rock Star Fan

Music, music everywhere, it's all wonderful to me,
In all my dreams I have longed to be a crazy Fratelli.
The White Stripes is a band I like,
They're super smashing brill
Not like those girls from Girls Aloud, who really sound quite shrill!
I'd love to see the Plain White Tees,
They're so cool they could freeze!
And when they're on the radio,
I go so weak at the knees!
I'd really love to go to V,
That muddy, muddy place,
All my favourite bands are there,
They really are so ace!

Lucinda Wilks (12)
Painsley Catholic College

The World For The Future

More chocolate every day,
A free world to roam and play,
No chavs in cars with thumping beats,
More shooting stars above our streets.

Three wishes a week would be a dream,
And a purple sky from a laser beam,
Dogs with smiles, rabbits that talk,
Supersonic shoes when I go for a walk.

A big clean smile and strong white teeth,
A mascara that doesn't run and blotch underneath,
Hair that's silky smooth with a groovy new style,
No more colds and illnesses which make me feel vile.

Family and friends always there,
Always loving and ready to care,
My future world just needs to be,
My family, friends and me, me, me!

Natalie Torr (12)
Painsley Catholic College

Through The Eyes Of My Mum

Waking up in the morn
Having a great big yawn.
Getting ready to go out
Rushing all about.
Kids get up what a bore
Come downstairs and yawn some more
Going out to see my friends
What a way for the week to end.
Going out to treat them all
Am going to the shopping mall.
Still at the shopping mall buying toys for them all.
Going to school they think it's cruel.

Jakob Pickthorne (11)
Painsley Catholic College

Through The Eyes Of The Sky

You might think I am just the sky,
There's more to me that meets the eye.
I watch the world each night and day,
I watch the people laugh and play.
I see the rich, who have it all,
I see the poor who wish for more.
I own the clouds, I own the sun,
Wait there's more, I own the stars.
All of the planets, even Mars.
When you are gazing up at me,
I wonder what you really see.
A pure blue sky just like the ocean,
The clouds drift in a soothing motion.
A dark grey sky all full of fear,
You see a storm come rumbling near.
I am the sky, you can't change that,
I am the eye of the Earth, and that's a fact.

Kimberley Ball (12)
Painsley Catholic College

Through The Eyes Of My Dog

I wake up in the morning
I bark until my owners get up
When they get up
They let me out
I chase the rabbit
Even though it's in a cage
I come back in for my breakfast
I go back out
And chase the rabbit for most of the day
I come back in
Have my tea
And go to bed.

Oliver Good (11)
Painsley Catholic College

World For Future

W hy is the world a big big place
O r is it because of the human race
R eligion or colour should not matter
L ive your dreams today
D o not let them shatter.

F un, fun, fun
O r let's run, run, run
R elax, unwind and always be kind

F orget all the bad things and
U nderstand the good
T he world together sings
U sually they would
R emember to treat all people the same
E ach and everyone, that is the game.

Mark Fallows (11)
Painsley Catholic College

A World For The Future

A world for the future
Where there's no need for spite
A world for the future
Where there's no need to fight.

A world for the future
Where there's love and not war
A world for the future
Where there's no needy or poor.

A world for the future
Full of faith and hope
A world for the future
Maybe everyone would cope.

Beth Foster (13)
Painsley Catholic College

A World For The Future

A world for the future
Where life isn't the same.
Where death and destruction
Isn't a game.

Where if you look different
Others won't stare.
You can act like yourself
And others won't care.

Where instead of ourselves
We'll think about others
And we don't fight and argue
With our sisters and brothers.

Where different colours and genders
Have the same rights
And envy and jealousy
Don't cause massive fights.

Molly Boughey (12)
Painsley Catholic College

Sand

Slipping, sliding, through my fingers,
Gritty and warm, soft as a lamb.
Scoop it up and let it fall,
It's the sand on the beach.

But when I get wet, it goes all sticky,
All on my legs, my arms, my hands.
Gooey and oozy, like golden syrup,
It's the sand on the beach.

In my hair, in my mouth,
Everywhere I look there's sand!
In my eyes, in my ears,
It's the sand on the beach.

Hannah Cooper (13)
Painsley Catholic College

Through A Lonely Kitten's Eyes

My little friend called Moonlight.
Is soft and cuddly,
Cute and cheeky,
Affectionate and loveable!

My little friend called Moonlight,
Was lonely and weak,
Small and unloved,
Matty and timid
That was until I found him!

My little friend called Moonlight,
Is now a big and cuddly pussy,
He's sweet and strong,
He's loved and happy now with me.

My little friend called Moonlight,
He's fat and fluffy,
He's loud and loving
Oh how I wish I was him!

Elizabeth Kaine (12)
Painsley Catholic College

Through The Eyes Of Paris Hilton!

I wake up to fresh toast topped with caviar,
With aqua-minerale, the whole world according to moi,
Stepping downstairs I slap on some clothes,
What I'll wear, nobody knows,
Out on a shopping spree,
The gorgeous shoes of the world are all for me,
When I'm at parties,
I'm eating golden Smarties,
With a diet like mine at dinner,
I'll never get any thinner,
But to be an heiress it comes with blood,
So you can start by packing your face with mud!

Laura Woodroffe (12)
Painsley Catholic College

Blind

My eyes are dim I cannot see.
I've never seen my family.
Day and night seem the same to me.
But I still live happily.

My ears make up for my failing eyes.
I hear things that others don't.
I can tell by their tone people's lies
The tales I could tell but I won't.

I've never seen a football match
But I know that scoring roar.
I've never seen a cricketer make a stunning catch.
But I've heard the groan when the ball hits the floor.

I only know it's sunny by the warmth on my face
I don't know what people mean when they say it's foggy.
I can tell when it's windy as I hear it blowing things all over the place.
I can also tell when it's rained because the ground feels really boggy.

I have a dog and in his ways he's really funny.
As well as my best friend he also helps me with my lack of sight.
He loves to lie on my bed while I rub his tummy.
He sleeps at the end of my bed every night.

Christopher Hughes (11)
Painsley Catholic College

Through The Eyes Of A Chair

Being a chair isn't that easy,
People sitting on you, people moving you.
You'd be surprised how painful it is.
At the start when the children come in.
I pray a small person will sit on me.
In-between lessons I get a break when I can rest.
But then another person will pick me up and take one to
                                    another classroom
Where I sit and hope the classroom doesn't get used.

Daniel Allen (13)
Painsley Catholic College

Through The Eyes Of A Nit

In a towering forest of hair,
We lay our eggs while singing our songs.
This poor boy doesn't know we are there,
Because of us he gives off a pong.

Now the time has come, to run, run, run,
Time to escape that nit killing brush!
My friends are lifted into the sun,
Jump to the next head oh what a rush!

Time to build the next colony,
Hours of egg laying yet again.
After days I got my family,
But now the acidy shampoo rain.

I turned and ran but what a mistake
They've got us with the shampoo and comb.
The shampoo was now an acid lake,
My friends fell in and turned into foam.

Josh Jones (13)
Painsley Catholic College

Vivienne Westwood

Wondering round thinking what to make,
Vivienne Westwood, my second cousin once removed
Drawing and sewing, saying 'That's rubbish' or 'That's boring'
Or 'That's not bad.'

How does she do it, all day thinking about what to make?
It's amazing, the things she makes,
Perfume and clothes, it would make me shake!
She has so many ideas if she doesn't use some she'll explode.

But I'd love to do what she does, I'm so amazed,
I'd like to plot and sew to perfection
And my fans would be dazed,
With all the things I've made!

Holly O'Rourke (11)
Painsley Catholic College

I Am A Mouse

I am a mouse,
I live in a house,
By a table in a little hole dark.
I love to eat cheese while I'm on my bed of leaves
But I have to look out for a trap!
I have a happy little life
In my happy little home
But there's one problem for me
The cat! The cat!
Says 'I think I smell a rat'
As he peers through my little hole door,
He chases me around,
Even tries to get me drowned,
But that's no problem for me!
I am fast! I am fast!
I never come last,
So look out cats, you're a thing of the past!

Bromwyn Goodwin (11)
Painsley Catholic College

In The Eyes Of . . . An Interactive Whiteboard

Every day I am used,
Being touched all around my body
With every child in the room
Watching me
Sometimes the children don't watch me
And the teacher has to shout.

I wish that I could just be left alone in peace.
People also touch my friend, he is called the projector.
If he is not on nobody touches me
I dread the day that someone touches me with a normal pen!
I will be with all of my broken relatives.

Adam Khalifa (12)
Painsley Catholic College

A World In The Future

A world in the future with no hate and war
A world in the future where no one is poor
I hope it's a place where creatures can roam
I hope it's a place where people call home.

A world in the future where everyone's free
A world in the future filled with hope and glee
I hope it's a place with love and peace
I hope it's a place where hatred will cease.

A world in the future without crime and drugs
A world in the future without vicious thugs
I hope my wishes for a better world come true
Because then it will be a better place for me and for you.

Gabriella Cordall (12)
Painsley Catholic College

A World For The Future

A world for the future, no violence, hate or spite,
A world for the future where people are polite.
A world for the future where happy people live,
A world for the future how much would you give?
A world for the future where animals can roam,
A world for the future somewhere we really can call home.
A world for the future where equality is real,
A world for the future where everybody has a meal.
A world for the future where everyone has fun,
A world for the future a million miles from here,
A world for the future is it something we shall fear.
A world for the future we'll just have to wait and see,
A world for the future now that's the place for me.

Jessica Cooper (13)
Painsley Catholic College

The Meaning Of Life

The meaning of life
Is only a human quest
It could be found in a goblet of fire
Or in your mates string vest.

I dreamt this secret
But I cannot tell
As the Reaper will send me
Straight to Hell.

Everyone will know this secret for sure
When your last breath is taken and your heart beats no more.

When it's too late
To undo the past
A broken heart, a poison letter
It's too late now to make things better.

The meaning of life
Is known by more than a few
All who have passed away now
They will soon be speaking with you.

Your voice is now only a whisper
The only ear available is the fetcher of souls
AKA The Grim Reaper

A bright light, the pearly gates have opened
So come on hop it
Now the meaning of life will be a daily topic.

Daniel Boot (12)
Painsley Catholic College

Through The Eyes Of A Dog

My name is Alfie
And I am three
I like to run
I think it's fun.

Everyone thinks that I am cute
But really I'm a little brute
I can run really fast
I for sure won't come last.

I love to be in my home
There's always a place for me to roam
I always find lots of things
Especially beef sandwich fillings.

My owner is really great
With him I'll always have a mate
His name is Tim
And I love being with him.

So now you know what it's like for me
I'll go on a walk and get dirty
Talk to you soon
Maybe at 12 noon.

Adam Cordall (12)
Painsley Catholic College

A Young Person's Life

I love to watch the days go by
Monday, Tuesday, they seem to fly
Summer's here, it brings such fun
Winter comes goodbye the sun
I love to play with all my friends
I hate it when it has to end
Time goes by so fast and quick
It sometimes makes me feel quite sick
But life is something to enjoy
So make the most, all girls and boys.

Sarah Dudley (13)
Painsley Catholic College

A World For The Future

Don't you ever wish that the world could change,
Or do you think it should stay the same?

That different people would agree and abolish war,
Or to make life easier, have electronic doors.

Maybe all people would get on,
Perhaps sprouts should taste like bonbons.

Willing robots would come to your every need,
Or that animals could self feed.

Everybody would be happy with each other,
When you're old you would still have a caring mother.

People in poor countries could eat clean food,
Or that you would never get angry and go into a mood.

I think that the world should change in ways you may agree,
So that it's a better place to live in for you and me.

Kate Harding (12)
Painsley Catholic College

Through The Eyes Of Cheeky Charlie

Cheeky Charlie is my name and being naughty is my game!
I hate working all day long, it really makes me pong!
So I buck them of my back but then I get a really hard smack!
I am lazy, am fat, my rider's just got a brand new riding hat.

In the morn I eat my corn, it makes me want to yawn,
My mouth is as big as the dawn!
It is yummy in my tummy, it's smelly a bit of my mummy!
I love bucking people off
The flies really naff me off!

Luisa Thorley (11)
Painsley Catholic College

This Poem Is About Stevie Wonder

I wake up to feel the brightness of the sun
I try to pour my tea but it ends up burning me.
I go to my concert and I hear the crowd sing
'There is superstition writing on the wall.'
When all I can do is sing with them wearing my bling, bling.
When my fans sing with me I say, 'Come on everybody'
'Signed, sealed, delivered.'
After my concert I have a drink not knowing what it is -
All this happens because I was born blind and cannot see
But I am grateful at least I can sing.

Oliver Stott (11)
Painsley Catholic College

Through The Eyes Of Bess The Dog

Oh yey dinner
I love having my food
All crunchy with big chunks of meat.
I love walks too
Going through the lovely countryside with my owner.
Thing I hate are baths,
Bubbles and water horrible!
But what I hate the most is
When my owner goes out and I've got no one to
                                        play with.

Mollie Smith (11)
Painsley Catholic College

Through The Eyes Of Hannah Montana

I am more than just one girl,
Me to control two lives,
Two ambitions,
One secret,
And two friends to trust.

My life as a pop star,
So hard to keep inside me,
Can't take it much longer,
Need to tell someone,
But I can't, must stay inside, not to be revealed.

I am a rock star,
Any teenager's dream,
I am known to many people,
I have another side of me,
A regular teenage girl, underneath the wig.

Emily Scarlett (12)
Painsley Catholic College

In The Eyes Of Ricardo Fuller!

Scoring goals to get the crowd roaring
Getting them on the edges of their seats.
My aim is to show skill and tactics
To keep my team in the heats.
I'm sure no one can call this boring
When they see me scoring.
The linesman puts his flag up
But I know I'm not offside.
But the way football is going
So many rules apply.
The atmosphere at the stadium is
Electric no one would believe being
A footballer is every boy's 'dream'.

Lee Minor (11)
Painsley Catholic College

Through The Eyes Of A Dolphin

I used to love speeding through the ocean,
And jumping really high,
I used to love being able to see the bottom of the sea,
But now my life has changed,
And my future might only be tomorrow,
If pollution doesn't stop and poachers being around,
You might not see me anymore.

Once I was a happy dolphin being wild and free,
Until I saw my extinction around the corner,
How can I die when I am the star of the sea?
Why does everything have to be dumped in the sea?
And how can they sell me for money?
When I am just an unhappy dolphin,
I was once the happiest mammal around,
But now I must be the saddest dolphin.

Nicola Campbell (11)
Painsley Catholic College

Through The Eyes Of Sky, My Little Sister

I hate waking up early in the morning,
When the sun is dawning
I look at the clock,
When I put on my sock!
After 9 o'clock
I have got on my sock!
When I go downstairs I want to go to bed again,
But after waking up I always bang my head!

I love to eat my toast
Especially before my roast!
I get in the car to go to school
Which is totally uncool!

Amy Hurst (11)
Painsley Catholic College

Talkin' 'Bout My Generation Open Your Eyes

What do you see when you walk down the street
A drunken man, a liar, a cheat?
What do you see when you walk down the hill,
A huddle of hoodies, ready to kill?
What do you smell as you walk to the fair?
A lung full of fumes, hangs thick in the air.

What do you see when you walk down the street?
Smiling children with music in their feet.
A lollipop lady who beams with pride,
As her precious charges are kept safe at her side.
What do you smell as you walk to the fair?
Hot dogs and happiness, hangs thick in the air.

Who do you see as you walk down the street?
The gymslip mum, her kids at her feet.
The homeless man with his begging bowl,
Give him a quid and he'll sell you his soul.
What do you smell as you walk to the fair?
Sweat, blood and tears, but nobody cares.

What do you see as you walk down the street?
Every day people, both young and old,
Some good, some bad, with tales to be told,
Of how life was better, in the good old days,
And how these young 'uns need to change their ways.

Open your eyes as you walk down the street,
Hold your head up high, don't look at your feet!
The size zero model, thin with starvation,
We all want to be her, that's my generation.
Reveal magazine has replaced the Bible,
Say the wrong thing and they'll sue you for libel.

What do you see as you walk down the street?

Robert Morris (13)
Painsley Catholic College

Sleepy Hollow

Sleepy Hollow lies there almost dead
A tree of such beauty once, now a tree of ugliness.
Her branches broken, some on the floor,
And her roots twisting in all directions.
It's fall and not many leaves are left on Sleepy Hollow
Her own body of leaves lies around her as she stays still
And gently swaying in the wind
She moans if you listen carefully
I wish I could help.
The cemetery was such a lovely place but now it's cold and dark
She hates it there. I know she does.
She's told me.
I love her, she's my best friend,
And she does speak but only to me.
They are thinking about chopping her down.
They won't, I won't let them
Them are what me and her call them.
We hate them so much, we don't say their names!
I sometimes cry and so does she.
She tells me not to be sad,
She comforts me and I comfort her!
I have my problems, a lot actually and I feel alone so does she.
So we join as one to help and comfort each other.
People think I am crazy, I don't talk to anyone apart from my family,
                                                                a bit,
And that's who I mean by no one, no one!
I cry, because of them, them are selfish.
I could not stop them this time!
I am so sorry! I love you and I will never forget you!

Anna Kilgannon (11)
Painsley Catholic College

Today's Genration

Today's generation
Is a strange little thing
We live in a world
Full of electrical things
Computers and mobiles
Games like 'The Sims'
Facebook and Bebo
Where strangers are friends.

No longer at Christmas
Are simple gifts had,
Our presents do nothing
But confuse mums and dads.
Where once we would set up
The trains and the tracks,
We now just press buttons
Or plug in our jacks.

Despite all the hi-tech
And gizmos and things,
I have to admit,
That I'm missing something.
When winter nights come,
And I'm finished making a mess,
There's nothing that beats
A good game of chess!

Ellis Maguire (13)
Painsley Catholic College

Through The Eyes Of My Dog

My dog is called Betty
Her favourite food is mince
It's very soft and crunchy
It doesn't like dog chocolate
It loves water!

She hates having baths
She always splashes and kicks
All the water and makes a dreadful mess!
She hates being brushed.

She likes walking
Mostly enjoys going to parks
And being free of her lead.
She doesn't like her black leather collar
With her name on 'Betty'.

She also doesn't like being on her own,
Starts to moan and puts her claws on the door
Trying to get out!
But she never does.

She's brown and white
And very fluffy.
She is my best dog, I've ever had
Woof!

Chloe Moore (11)
Painsley Catholic College

Through The Eyes Of My Mum

I like to be organised
I like to be neat and tidy
I like everything to be perfect
I like everything in its place.

I like Emmerdale
I like Coronation Street
I like EastEnders
I like peace and quiet.

I hate cooking
I hate cooking horrible things
I hate cooking roast dinners
I hate cooking anything.

I hate cleaning
I hate cleaning the toilets
I hate cleaning the dishes
I hate cleaning other people's mess.

Madalaine Forrester (11)
Painsley Catholic College

Milly

Milly is silly
When she chases the chickens
And when she has a
Bath it's such a laugh
Eating food it's everywhere
Playing with toys
Throwing a stick
And crushing it
Throwing a ball, throw
Some more.

Mark Finney (11)
Painsley Catholic College

Kids Today

Ppl think we r all bad nooz
But they shud try be in in r shooz
Sum ov us aint all tht bad
The rep we get can make us sad.

We dnt try 2 frite nd scare
But ther r sum who r a nitemare
Kidz like me r nice and kind
Better try keep tht in mind!

Dnt b scared tht we will bite
But sadly those ov us just mite
Just make sure you cut us slack
Then respect will come rite bk.

Joseph Unyolo (13)
Painsley Catholic College

Flossy The Cat

My name is Flossy,
My fur is white,
I go out on the prowl,
When it is dark at night,
Then I look for a mouse,
And then bring it to the house,
And when I go back to the house,
I can start to eat my juicy mouse,
My mouse tastes very tasty,
It tastes just like pastry,
I wish I had some beef gravy,
Next time,
Just maybe.

Aaron Booth (11)
Painsley Catholic College

If I Had A Power

If I had a power to make plants grow,
I would go to a place where they don't know.
How to farm their land and cure their meat,
I'd make it so they had enough to eat.

If I had a power to cool things down,
I would stop the heat going round and round.
I would stop the Earth getting too warm,
So that we could all live 'til the next dawn.

If I had a power to change the weather,
It would be right for the place forever and ever.
The weather would be fine day in and day out,
There would be water in Africa and not so much drought.

If we could all have the powers we all desired,
The world wouldn't be in danger and tired.
We would all be happy and peaceful and smile,
But if that ever happens it will take a long while.

Siobhan Hunt (13)
Painsley Catholic College

The Future Is Wild

The future world could be anything
It could be bombarded by meteorites
Or invaded by aliens
The future world could be right

Lightsabers or laser guns
Aliens or clones
Vampires or werewolves
Nobody knows.

People might be living in space
Hover cars or flying bikes
Human robots or cybermen
The future could be bright

So you can see that the future is *wild*.

Karsen Poon (11)
Painsley Catholic College

My Generation

My generation is great,
No worries about money
Full of gadgets and laughs with a mate
Jokes on the school bus, so funny
Life always seems so sunny.

My generation is fun,
Working hard all day at school
Then messing about in the sun
Prevents us becoming a fool
And sitting on the dunce's stool.

My generation is loud
Whilst relaxing in our gang
We stand out from the crowd
On the street corners we hang
Breaking something causing a bang.

Ryan Molloy (13)
Painsley Catholic College

No One To Be With

I have no one to be with
I'm very alone
My owner has dumped me in this horrid home
All the dogs bark at night, you can't get to sleep
All you can do is cry and weep
The dog orphanage never looks after us
When I'm hungry I don't get fed and when
I'm thirsty, I don't get a drink
I wish someone would care and play with me
I'm very upset and alone
I wish someone would take me home.

Gabriella Licata (11)
Painsley Catholic College

Just Another Kid Closer

Nana Betty was on a mission,
Her grandson was kidnapped whilst fishin'.
She had caught a whopper and was preoccupied,
When a man crept up from the other bank side.
He grabbed Alex, who jumped with surprise,
They left a note saying, 'You can pay the price'.

She was on her way after them,
On her scooter model fifty-six M.
'I may be old - but I'm still hard,
Because you yobs trashed my backyard!
Chasing after you night and day,
How dare you insinuate that I should pay!'

Meanwhile in a small Ford Fiesta,
Little Alex Boon was taking a siesta.
He was blindfolded, gagged and stuffed in the boot,
'You're not free unless we get paid some loot!'
There he crouched with a gun to his head,
His dreams were all smothered, choked and red.

He awoke abruptly as they rounded a bend
And continued his prayers for a quick clean end.
Well for what else was he supposed to pray?
There was little chance he'd live to see the light of day.
He'd seen the stories on the news,
Whilst his old nan knocked back the booze.

Maybe Nan'll get taken to court,
She'll get the blame oh no she could.
Mum and Dad I might see you soon
And my pet hamster Mr Racoon.
Please God be nice to me,
I wanted to live till fifty-three.

Alex Boon - no 321783,
How many more will it take for us to see?
'Just another kid' they'll say,
But it happens every day.

Naomi Tyers (13)
Painsley Catholic College

Don't We All Want To Be An Eco Warrior?

Global warming fiction or fact,
Is it our fault or nature's pact?
Do we act the way we should act?
Should our habits just be sacked?
Don't we all want to be an eco warrior?

Is our technology all that clever and good?
Are things we make misunderstood,
Cars and planes, plastic and wood,
All things we use in each neighbourhood,
Don't we all want to be an eco warrior?

The gas, petrol and diesel fumes,
These don't make the flowers bloom,
Clothes, make-up and nice perfume
Are these items just doom and gloom,
Don't we all want to be an eco warrior?

Nature's beauty being destroyed,
Can the hilltop views still be enjoyed?
Is Mother Nature getting annoyed
When all the fields and land are void?
Don't we all want to be an eco warrior.

So recycle those unwanted things,
Even those ancient shoes and rings,
Restore the splendour nature brings,
The melody that all the birds sing,
Don't we all want to be an eco warrior?

We have technology, we have our say,
Let's make a clear future day,
Where pure and green we portray,
Let's make that eco day today!
Let's all be Eco Warriors!

Martha Sowter (13)
Painsley Catholic College

Make A Difference

The world today is so unfair.
No one cares,
They don't care about those who are poor,
The people who are cut, wounded and sore.

People in the Third World country have nothing compared to us,
We can use anything; they can't even use a bus.
We should care about what they think and need,
Every day they try to make money by growing a seed.

We should make a difference, and help them
We need to make it a fairer life for them.
People die every day,
They are too poor to afford medicines, they are too poor to pay.

In Britain we can buy all the things we need
We always take the lead.
We control who gets what,
Poorer countries don't get much, others get a lot.

We should all be the same,
All equal and no one in pain.
We need to make a difference and think of others
After all they are sisters and brothers.

Nobody is different, so why should they be treated in a bad way.
They deserve their say.
We should all live in peace and not in war
We should all be happy and nobody should be poor.

If we make a difference the world can be a better place.

Emily Campbell (13)
Painsley Catholic College

Labels

Yobs and chavs stride through the town
Wearing gold chains, trackies and a cap as a crown.

The goths and greebos trundle up the street
Wearing heavy make-up and cursing everyone they meet.

The mad hippies are bouncing into the road
Making peace gestures with their finger code.

Preps and casuals natter their way to the park
They will sit there whittering until it goes dark.

Gangsters and hardcores are planning a fight
Which won't even take place until tomorrow night.

Emos are gloomily shuffling their feet
And then kicking the stones pulled loose from the concrete.

Rockers and drunks parading the alleys
Whilst jockeys and athletes race in the valleys.

Is this right? How can we be sure?
Is labelling people okay anymore?
The life that we are leading is our own choice
So let these people stand up, let us hear their voice
Not all want to be classed in gangs and mobs
But as individualised civilians - not just kids with big gobs
Don't judge anyone before you judge yourself
You may not have good fortune and you may not have good wealth
But that really doesn't matter, you're a human like me
And we are all a part of God's family!

Annabel Emery (13)
Painsley Catholic College

A Dog's Life

I once was loved, then my owner died,
Then I was cast out, down by the wayside.

I hit the ground, got covered with frost,
Yelped, looked up, realised I was lost.

As time passed by, I began to moan,
For the first time in my life, I was alone.

As the night wore on, it began to snow,
And then sure enough, a gale started to blow.

Later on, as cars whizzed by,
I lay down exhausted, ready to die.

As I started to shiver, and drift off to sleep,
I felt warm hands lift me to my feet.

They wrapped me in a blanket,
And gave me food to eat.

I was taken to a place where I could stay,
Full of dogs howling, every night and every day.

I was there for weeks, maybe more,
The spiked collar on my neck made it very sore.

One morning I awoke to the laughter of a child,
I began to run around, heart going wild.

Finally a family, looking for a dog,
I could see a way out, out of this fog.

'She looks lonely, let's take her home'
Said a girl, and there it was, the seed had been sown.

The parents agreed, put me in the car,
And took me home, which wasn't very far.

They gave me the name Shadow, which suited me fine,
Because I now had a family that was truly mine.

Izaak Bailey (13)
Painsley Catholic College

Her Last Words

Well this is goodbye my darling,
I hope you remember me with every starling
Which passing by this street
I leave you sitting in this seat.

This was never a superstitious homicide
We both know this is an adolescent suicide . . .
I'll take this gun, and shoot this bullet,
We sure ain't no Romeo and Juliet.

I was blinded by your fake heart
Now is your chance for that new start
You always said 'I'll love you till I die'
Well you shattered love into my eye.

Well can we settle this affair?
Now I'm gone you don't have to care
You won't see my white washed face
Or my bloodstained necklace.

Without me here to drag you down
There aren't oceans deep enough for you to drown
Maybe you'll keep the razor blades?
Well here's your answer in spades.

Watch sky above the coffin door
Pray it'll bleed above me
Just promise me one thing before I go?
Don't let them kill without a no?

Well this is goodbye my darling
I hope you remember me with every starling
Which passes by this street,
Those were her last words on this sheet . . .

Emily Hulme (13)
Painsley Catholic College

People

What do we think of people?
You say you love them,
And swear under the steeple,
That you'll never forget them.
But to most, that's just hypocrisy,
Why do we ignore those who are different?
Those who step out and aren't fussy?
Oh my God! You're different!
The stereotyped cults in their corners,
They, so perfect all the same.
Ha, look at the emos, all mourners.
Look at the chavs, they dress so lame.
Just because someone's different,
Doesn't mean they need harassment.
In fact the indifferent
They are the ones who give encouragement,
Are the ones who are much more interesting
Your hairstyle doesn't affect your personality.

Seb Morrell (13)
Painsley Catholic College

My Poem

Pure fresh air turned sour.
Ocean's water levels rising.
Lethal fumes.
Lethal gases.
Other living creatures dying.
Ultimate destruction will come.
Information given to stop using the car.
Ozone shaking, smashing, shattering.
New problems developing.

Stephen Phillips (11)
Painsley Catholic College

Kids These Days

Going out with friends
And major trends
The most popular things in my generation

Staying out late
Getting a nice date
The most popular things in my generation.

Going to towers
Having fun for hours
The most popular thing in my generation.

Getting ASBOS and causing trouble
Reducing civilisation to rubble
The most popular thing in my generation.

Drugs and fags
And dirty mags
The most popular thing in my generation.

Spending time with the family
And helping the old,
The least popular things in my generation.

Daniel Davis (13)
Painsley Catholic College

The Daily Trail

The cockerel crows at the crack of dawn,
As a blanket of dew spreads across the lawn.
The golden sun rises from above the hills,
While my pet goldfish wakes and sways his gills.
At Christmas the snowflakes dance and swirl,
As I hear the sound of laughter from a little girl.
At Easter the kids run with chocolate all over their face,
Their happiness is something that no one can replace.
When summer arrives in the middle of June,
We all jump up and down and sing a happy tune.

Rebecca O'Connor (11)
Painsley Catholic College

Music

Music over the years has changed a lot,
There's been reggae, pop, and lots, lots more.
My favourite music just has to be R'n'B
Especially Fergie!

Classical music is boring,
It's really depressing too,
I like jazz - I think it's cool,
It just makes me want to dance.

Pop is short for popular,
And means 'a range of different styles',
Reggae originated in Jamaica,
And was top in the 1970s.

Rap is very annoying
And is also known as hip hop,
The blues is really sad
And was started by the slaves.

Disco is so fab,
I love the disco balls!
English folk music is played on the guitar,
And loved by everyone!

Rhiannon Gibson (13)
Painsley Catholic College

My Generation

Don't drop the paper put it in the bin,
It would be an awful sin
Put the tins in a special box,
So it can be made into clocks
Plastic can be special too,
As it can make other things
Bright and blue
So don't drop litter on the floor,
As it is harmful to nature's call.

Megan Prins (11)
Painsley Catholic College

My Generation

I have a dog called Callie,
She always takes my socks,
She's really fast at running,
She climbs up all the rocks!

I have a dog called Callie,
She always takes my shoes.
She runs around the garden,
Then lies down for a snooze!

I have a dog called Callie,
She steals food out the bin.
She gets it all round her mouth,
And all over her chin!

I have a dog called Callie,
The cold she really loathes,
She runs up to my bedroom,
And hides under my clothes.

Her name it should be mischief,
She's such a cheeky hound,
But even though she's naughty,
She's worth a million pounds.

Rachelle Cooper (11)
Painsley Catholic College

Happiness

H appiness is a walk in the park,
A utumn leaves falling from trees,
P icking fresh strawberries from the fields,
P osing for photographs on the beach,
I ce cream and lollies on a hot day,
N othing to do but enjoy the sunshine,
E ating food from the barbecue,
S urrounded by good friends,
S nuggling up in bed after a really good day.

Jack Degg (11)
Painsley Catholic College

My Generation Through My Great Gran's Eyes

Discs, computers, megapixal, mouses and plugs,
When I was a girl there was vegetables to be dug.
Mobile phones, infra-red, blue tooth,
When I was a child it was all about truth.

Sundays were always a day of rest,
When we would dress in our Sunday best.
Singing on a Sunday while sat on a pew,
Now the background sounds of ringtones with texts to do.

Black and white televisions with the turn of a dial,
Now flatscreen TVs with a DVD file.
Huddies and astros, hair in a mess,
We'd have to go to church in our Sunday best.

From our atlas books that we studied for many a while,
Now my grandson clicks 'enter' on a Google file.
From the dentist torture, we had back then,
To the pearly white false teeth for a perfect smile.

Times do change every once in a while,
As I look back over the years,
I can but smile.

Callum Bradbury (11)
Painsley Catholic College

Generation

G ases and fumes
E ngulfing
N ature's work
E volution
R ipped
A part
T orn because of the
I nfinite
O ngoing, activity of human beings
N ever stopping, never thinking, never acting.

Tam Bowyer (11)
Painsley Catholic College

Untitled

I don't play kick the can,
Or hide-and-seek,
I think that would make me look like a total geek.

If I want to play tennis, or ride my scooter,
I get out my Nintendo Wii, it's a great computer.

No more knocking on doors, to go see my friends,
If I want to chat, I text a message that's the new trend.

No more going to discos, I don't do that,
I get out my PlayStation 2 and fancy dance mat.

Phones, iPods, emails, TV, laptops and my own mp3.

Gadgets and gismos, for these things I'm wishing
But I can't help but think, is there something missing?

Georgina Bailey (11)
Painsley Catholic College

My Generation

G eneration is all about the here and now
E veryone holds us back but we climb back up again
N aughty but nice we're all misunderstood
E verything suffers even if we can't see it
R acist terms are used behind our back
A re ways that we control
T oday is the day we can change the world
I nspiring ways we sometimes follow
O n this day we offer our thoughts to help us change
N othing ever comes from not changing.

Leah Machin (11)
Painsley Catholic College

My Generation

Technology today,
What would we do without?
We would get nowhere with no doubt,
There are computers and even electric scooters
We have iPods to listen to music on but it
Doesn't mean the record has gone.

Technology today
We have this great stuff but it doesn't mean we
Don't have to pay
We still have cars
And some believe there are aliens waiting in
The stars
We still have law but it doesn't mean to say
People aren't still poor.

Technology today what do you have to say?

Kieren O'Leary (11)
Painsley Catholic College

My Generation

My generation uses the iPod
Older generations think it's odd.

Phones are the 'next big thing!'
Better get the ringtone *'ding'*

Lots and lots of different things
High school, scary school, new term brings

Three cheers for my generation
Let's kick off with a celebration.

Rachel Sollitt (11)
Painsley Catholic College

When I Wake Up

When I wake up in the morning
I smell the fresh air
I say a morning prayer
Then I comb my hair.

I hear the birds tweeting
Then breakfast and wash
Always early never have to dash.

First on the bus
Always last off
Sit with my friends
And we always have a laugh.

When I'm at school
I see my cool new friends
They always have a smile for me
Because we're really good friends.

Nicholas Perkin (11)
Painsley Catholic College

My Generation

My generation is computer game time,
Dancing, singing, answering questions.
My generation is playing on the computer,
Football, cricket, all kinds of sport.
My generation is playing on games,
Car games, fighting games, it's all lots of fun.
My generation is having fun,
Switch on the computer and have a great time.
My generation is good not boring,
What fun it is in my generation.

Richard Williams (11)
Painsley Catholic College

The Future

The future holds things for you and me
The future holds things we can't see

It's staring us into the eyes
The box that holds a big surprise

Even when you are asleep
It's on your pillow packed and neat.

In the morning dreams are fading
And future box is there and waiting.

City towns are getting busy
But future box sits quiet but dizzy.

Future box counts down and down
Until the moment comes around.

Future box whispers a clue
To every single one of you.

Now here's a clue inside the clue
It will bring happiness to you.

But if you turn to abuse this power
It will be gone within an hour.

The powers will but take its time
But soon the magic won't be mine.

Now the box refused to speak
And then a noise, a crack, a creek.

The future box began to shake
And all the beings, tired - awake.

People rushed into the street
And long-lost loves began to meet.

Now the open box exists
It so kindly does assist.

A crowd of people gather around
'What about us?' they asked and frowned.

You were foolish and didn't listen
Soon you will receive your great present.

People stand with pride and joy
And ask in wondrous tongue

What is this power you give to us
And how long is it to last?

Love . . .

Kieran Carnwell (11)
Painsley Catholic College

One Small, Small Box

One small, small box
In the dark of the night
One red, red fox
Hears a squeal of fright
One tap at a door
Light appears fast
One will be here for sure
Help at last.

One small, small girl
Takes in the box
One little look inside
Thanks to the fox
One fluffy, fluffy little kitten
In a new home
One happy little girl
Who will never ever moan

There is a reason for life.

Alice Pattinson (11)
Painsley Catholic College

About Fay!

There was once a girl called Fay,
She sat at her desk and did her hair all day
Everyone used to say
What a beautiful girl that Fay!

She got A grades at school,
So her parents bought her a swimming pool.
Everyone used to say,
What a wonderful girl that Fay.

But underneath the make-up and the done-up hair,
There was a little sign saying handle with care.
Everyone used to say,
What a sensitive girl that Fay.

At school Fay was everyone's friend,
No one wanted their friendship with Fay to end.
Everyone used to say
What a lovely girl that Fay.

Fay was small and pretty
She loved to shop in the city
Everyone used to say
What a fashionable girl that Fay.

Now you've heard this poem we can all say
Fay was perfect in every single way.
Everyone used to say
What a perfect girl that Fay!

Rebecca Mountford (12)
Painsley Catholic College

Truly Mad!

I have a brother,
Who married his mother
Truly mad!
I have a friend,
Who drives me round the bend
Truly mad!
I have a cousin,
Who never stops buzzin'
Truly mad!
I have a mum,
Who is so dumb
Truly mad!
I have a dad,
Who is really, really sad
Truly mad!
I have a sister,
Who's so stupid I have never actually missed her
Truly mad!
I have an auntie,
Who's never had a party
Truly mad!
I have a nan,
Who drives a pink van
I have a mirror which I see myself in,
And ask myself is this my generation?
Of course it is because it is
Truly mad!

Georgia Thorley (11)
Painsley Catholic College

Generation

Oh how the world is changing . . .

As the time goes by the world is changing.
Technological advances have appeared like
Mushrooms after the rain.
We live in a computer age where computers are getting smaller
and faster.
Not so long ago computers were the size of a house,
But now they are so compact that you can fit one in your pocket!

Oh how the world is changing . . .

The environment is changing too.
Global warming, pollution are both altering the seasons
There is no more snow in some places,
So children cannot go sledging.
They are missing out on so much fun!

Oh how the world is changing . . .

We have so many different ways to travel.
In today's world we have fast cars, huge planes and big shops.
Not so long ago, Man's only dream was to travel on horseback,
But now Man can get to the stars in a rocket.

Oh how the world is changing . . .

Medicine has improved so much over the generation too.
Once upon a time man died from trivial diseases,
But we now have penicillin which has saved so many lives.
New advances have cured many diseases and even treated
test-tube babies.

The world is changing but for the better or for the worse?
Only future generations will be able to provide the answer!

Kacper Wozniak (11)
Painsley Catholic College

Tony Blair Vs Gordon Brown In The Eyes Of A Soldier

T is for Tony who faced the flack
O is for onwards, troops storming Iraq
N is for nuclear arms not found
Y is for yellow, the sand on the ground

B is for bloodshed, soldiers have died
L is for loved ones no one by their side
A is for artillery that's what went then
I is for injuries sustained by the men
R is for resignation before they come home again

V is for victory that no one has won
S for the soldiers in hot desert sun

G is for Gordon, he came after
O for opposition with jeers and laughter
R for retreat, troops pulling out
D for despair, in Iraq they shout
O for outraged that troops were sent there
N for a nation that lives in despair.

B is for boldness that he displays
R is for relishing his Great British ways
O pportunity to stand for election
W ill he succeed in this powerful selection?
N o one will know of his next direction.

Thomas Baskeyfield (11)
Painsley Catholic College

Monday Blues

Roses are red, I'm feeling blue,
What's a kid like me supposed to do?
Phone's out of credit, I'm wearing a frown,
Cos the PlayStation's broke and my brother's beating me down.
What's a kid like me supposed to do?
When I'm still stuck at school and the bus has gone too!

Callum Pegg (11)
Painsley Catholic College

The Abandoned Dog,The Abandoned Pets

I am all alone suffering the cold
Holding my fears trying to be bold
Watching litter fly past my nose
The loud horrible noises of the dreaded crows
I wait consistently for my loving owner
But I realised I got chucked out cos I am only a loner
My paws feel numb and my legs ache
I sleep all night and don't want to awake
To yet another day of misery.

We sit here huddling each other
Cos we're family, sister and brother
Penny the parrot doesn't understand what's going on
But the rest of us do our love we have none
We soon will starve and pass away from thirst
If our owners didn't dump us we'd still be family from birth
The moments we've been through and this is the end
Our owners have fooled us and now not our friend.

Danni McCormack (11)
Painsley Catholic College

Generation

G eneration is our lives now
E veryone needs to see our generation, how?
N ow everyone needs to work together
E veryone, let's make Earth last forever!
R ewind to the world's beginning
A nd just think, were any of us living?
T he best thing about all of this
I is that we are part of all of this
O ne and all are very special,
N ow I'm proud to say 'Our generation!'

Charlie Loughran (11)
Painsley Catholic College

Talkin' 'Bout My Generation

I'm a baby, so what!
I'm big enough to get out my cot.
I have a mum and a dad
Plus a brother, he ain't bad
In my world, everything is tall,
So I have to reach up, for my ball.
Mum is the person, who makes my food,
Milk or mush I get to choose.
I like to drink milk from my cup,
Sometimes I drink too much so I throw up.
Being a baby is really cool,
Cos you don't go to school!

Amy McKenna (11)
Painsley Catholic College

Talkin' 'Bout My Generation

My generation is PlayStation 3, Nintendo Wii,
My generation has all the same problems,
Global warming threatens us all,
Our carbon footprints grow all together,
My generation is a generation like no other,
My generation grows together, while the bleak future grows
Before us,
We improve and better ourselves as one.

Sam Tyers (11)
Painsley Catholic College

Talkin' 'Bout My Generation

A racing driver, that's the life for me.
Lewis Hamilton, that's who I'd like to be!
His concentration would need to be immense
As the countdown to the race is about to commence.
The race has started, off they blast,
Each one hoping they won't finish last.
On they travel at tremendous speed
The most skilled and able will take the lead.
Receiving valuable instructions on his radio,
About an obstruction that occurred a lap a go.
The safety car now joins the lap.
Everyone must now follow this chap.
All the drivers, brake, brake, brake.
There is no opportunity to overtake
Into the pits, the crew fetch fuel
Back out they go, to continue their duel.
Heading towards the chequered flag,
Another race firmly in the bag.
The champion begins his reign,
He celebrates on the podium with champagne.
How can I fulfil a dream?
Gain a place in his team!

Liam Kelly (12)
Painsley Catholic College

Machines

The future, the future, what a wonderful place.

Buzzing and beeping from all the new hover cars,
Wish, wish, as they pass you by.

Chit, chat, chit, chat, from all the new robots,
Nothing can stop them not even a plug.

No jobs to be found, no money to earn,
Machines have taken over, but it's not their turn!

Zoe Hurst (13)
Painsley Catholic College

Step Into The Spotlight

Step out of the door
One heel on the floor
Cameras flash I shield my eyes
I hide away the window to my mind.

A sheet of ice unknown
A fake personality full grown
Billions of eyes turn my way,
What could I ever say?

I'm pushed to the foreground
I can't turn the tables round
Shaking all over I don't let it show
Just hide the fear and go with the flow.

Smile and wave just chat away
Lose myself for another day
Can't step out, can't stay in,
Who am I really? How can I win?

They don't care what I think, they don't care what I feel
I'm what they want me to be they don't care if it's real
I'm a person not a picture but who would ever know
A prisoner in my own mind, I can't let myself go.

A celebrity you think that nothing compares?
But would you swap your life for theirs?

Lizzie Casey (11)
Painsley Catholic College

Blind!

B lind is dark, cold, boring and lifeless
L ight has gone, run away to a distant land
I mages are black like dark rain clouds
N obody can imagine the darkness of blind
D arkness has come, light has gone, blind!

James Smith (11)
Painsley Catholic College

The Future

The future is a mystery,
To them we are history,
In the future, they have the force,
Weapons like lasers, lightsabers of course.
Hoverboards lift you in the air,
Ride a spaceship if you dare.
In the future there are still wars,
New sets of rules and new laws,
In the future there are new names,
But there is still Tom, Jake and James,
The new Prime Minister is called McGregg,
He has a pet that would eat your leg,
In the future they still pray,
Hope you don't get killed by the heat ray.
Now I stop my poem for a future dream,
Hopefully I don't get shot by a laser beam.

Yasmin Hurst (11)
Painsley Catholic College

Mr Fox

I am running as fast as I can
Away from the dog and the man
I ran through the fence and over the gate
Where I saw my red fox mate.
I told him to run into the fields
I raced my way through the grass
And past the mole
Into my dark hole
There I was home again
Away from the dog and the man.

Bradley Moult (11)
Painsley Catholic College

Through Someone's Eyes

All I can see is black and white
I have got stripy skin and fur
My surroundings are jungle and savannah.

I have a huge dinner every week
I cook them myself
I also have wild vermin.

People hunt me for my skin
I kill them when I get frustrated
I hate it when they have loads of weapons.

My favourite things to do are:
To kill
To hunt
To roar!

Sean Hullah (11)
Painsley Catholic College

Homeless

H is for homeless, no place to stay
O is for owning but nothing to own
M is for moving, moving on all the time
E is for emotions, sad and alone
L is for loving, wanting a family to love
E is for endless nights spent all alone
S is for summer, no holiday to go on
S is for sadness, without a home.

Joanna Beard (11)
Painsley Catholic College

Hunt Of Moss Side

The 5am alarm signals
The start of another morn
The streets of Manchester await
Quiet, dark and forlorn.

Walk towards me bathroom
To give meself a wash
Prepare for what today may bring
To earn meself more dosh.

It's tough being a bobby,
In 1973
The streets are full of scumbags
And they all get sent to me.

Put me flares on, get me cuffs
Spark up the day's first fag
Drive to work in the old Cortina
With me snapping in me bag.

I am greeted by the custody sarge
Handing over a drunk
'What else went on last night?' I ask
To make the cell doors clunk.

The miners are on strike again
So there'll be trouble there
A lad of mine got glassed last week
He said their pay was fair.

Walk into the canteen
For me morning bowl of flakes
Radio's playing that song again
T Rex's 'Heaven Sakes'.

DI Tyler is on duty
He's been dealing with a car thief
Incident came in last night
Gave Sam a load of grief.

Told 'em time and time again
These interviews need taping
They sent us these cassette things
This department needs shaping.

Home time is here at last
We're all off down the pub
To share a pint and the trials of a day
In the life of DCI Hunt.

In 2007 the bobbies will think life's rough
But the law of my generation
Now that's what I call tough!

Eleanor Smith (12)
Painsley Catholic College

Generation

Blind people, blind people
Use their dogs as sight people,
Blind people, blind people
Use their sticks to find people.

Blind people, blind people,
Use their ears to hear people,
Blind people, blind people,
Use the Braille to read.

Blind people, blind people
Use dark glasses to see people,
Blind people, blind people
Use their touch to find.

Blind people, blind people,
Use alarms to do things,
Blind people, blind people
Are just like you and me people.
Blind people, blind people.

Rachel Roberts
Painsley Catholic College

Our Generation

Why are we in this generation?
People say 'Why weren't I born in the next generation?'
We are born throughout time
Our time is now.

We have to make our lives last forever,
Some people next generation will be stars,
Some might be in a factory,
But some might have nothing.
No matter what happens we stay together as one.
We stick together, win together, and as time goes by
We will always stay in this generation.

The future might be brilliant,
But now is even better,
The past's have been good,
But still now is the best.

We are together
We are one
We are the world
We are this generation.

Rhianne Sutton (11)
Painsley Catholic College

What The Future Holds

Truth be told
I worry what the future holds,
Will it be good, will it be bad?
No one knows!
Will it be happy, will it be sad?
Will we be rich, will we be poor?
No one knows
Will we live in comfort?
Will we live in poverty?
Nobody knows what the future holds!

Tom Plant (11)
Painsley Catholic College

Beckham Pressure

The match begins
It's time to play
The crowd want wins
Without delay.

Kick-off and we win the ball
Down to the penalty box time to shoot
Oh no foul, the forward took a fall
It's now time for my Adidas boot.

Now my team and country are depending on me
The wall is ready, run forward and aim
Bend it like Beckham - I'd love to guarantee
Yes it's in the net - another moment of fame.

Beckham's the hero again today
I wish it was like this every time I play
It's great when things go right
But being blamed for defeat gives me a fright.

Daniel Capper (11)
Painsley Catholic College

Spiders

Spiders, spiders,
Are good hiders,
No matter what you do.

They spin their webs,
At good revs,
Even in your shoe.

They're small and weak,
But do not creak,
When crawling across the floor.

They thrive in the cold,
They're difficult to hold,
They can even squeeze under the door!

Connor Hardisty (12) & Alex Hardisty (13)
Painsley Catholic College

Computer's Wish

C omputer is my name and there is one thing I want to be
O ff why do you never turn me off, it is all I want?
M ust you always stare at me, why can't you leave me alone?
P lease just let me rest for a couple of weeks
U nderstand that all I want is some peace and quiet
T ell me why you want to stare at me forever
E nd the torment and turn me off for once
R esent is all I feel in my hard drive for you
S o please find it in your heart and turn me off.

W hy didn't you turn me off when I asked you?
I pleaded for so long and you didn't listen
S o I'll tell you again, please turn me off
H elp me to rest I can't do it on my own, so turn me off.

Samuel Stephens (11)
Painsley Catholic College

The Orphanage

O rphans from far and wide come to the orphanage
R ight from the time that they were born
P eople come from around the world to see what they can find
H oping to see a boy or girl
A nyone who they could love
N o one could help but fall for their innocent little faces
A fter all they have nothing at all
G od could help to make it better
E ven though it could be worse, some don't even have food
                                                    or water.

Jessica Miller (12)
Painsley Catholic College

Next Generation

My next generation has been waiting for a while
I've had so many medical notes they come pile after pile.

I'm getting so many pains in my back,
It's like I've been carrying a very heavy sack.

My turn is over and life is to end,
But I wish that'll mend.

My generation is ending soon,
It will probably end by tomorrow noon.

May I say I'll live forever
But at this rate I will never.

My time is up, time to say goodbye,
It's my turn to die.

Adam Peaty (12)
Painsley Catholic College

A World For The Future

W ish, I wish for world peace
O h, it is so unfair for some people
R acist remarks have been said
L ong ago, it was even worse
D arkness there was, in the olden times.

P eace, will it ever come
E nd this now, while we still can
A mazing how many deaths there have been from racist remarks
C oloured or not coloured, it does not matter
E verlasting peace, that is what we wish for.

Bradley Finney (11)
Painsley Catholic College

I Wonder What It Would Be Like . . . ?

Walking down the red carpet
Graffiti wherever I go
Lots of celebrities to meet
I can't believe how much I glow
Having fancy dinners, bon appetit
Now it's time for my show
Look Ashley Tisdale's on the front row seat.

Being asked on a date
VIP tickets
Uh-oh I'm late
I forgot I hate cricket
Ahh, I'm in a state
Yeah! He made the first wicket.

I love my dreams
How I wish they would never end
I wonder what it would be like to 'beam'
Stand out in the crowd and make new friends
Imagine what it would be like through the eyes
Of a celebrity.

Charlotte Goldstraw (11)
Painsley Catholic College

I Dream

I dream of a future where the world is at peace
I dream of a future where the animals run free
Imagine a world as pure as crystal waters
Imagine a world that is full of hope, love and dreams
I see a future full of thick black smoke
I see a future full of conflict
Where dreams are shattered
Where hearts are broken
I know my dreams will never come true
The future I see is only too true.

Zoë Darbyshire (13)
Painsley Catholic College

Through The Eyes Of . . . Getting Bullied

I don't know why
I don't know how
All I can do is stand alone
And take the pain
They hit, they kick
Why kick me
Because I'm weak?
They all do it for some fun
I want to know why
It's something I can't discover
I want to know why but all I can do
Is stand alone and put together
The clues and then watch them get
Washed away in my mind and become
A thing of the past something
That I can only remember
They still do it and I wonder when they
Will stop it could be a day, a month or a year
    Or forever.

Alex Green (11)
Painsley Catholic College

A World For The Future

Stop the war
Stop the fights

Stop the poverty
Stop injustice

Bring in peace
Bring in love

Bring in fair play
Bring in justice.

Stephen Sammons (12)
Painsley Catholic College

I Wish And Wish I Could Fly!

I wish and wish I could fly,
Just like a bird up high in the sky
Up and up I go,
Just like a plane that isn't very low.

Up as high as I could be,
All the wonders I can see
Up in the breezy air
But really do I care?

I'm flying, I'm flying
Now do you think I'm sighing?
All the wonders I can see
Up as high as I could be.

I love it up here,
Everything is so clear,
I'm not sighing,
I'm flying, I'm flying!

Charlotte Hubble (11)
Painsley Catholic College

Ronaldinho

He's visited Rio De Janerio
And his name is Ronaldinho
He plays for Barcelona
Enric Masip is the owner
He's played in the World Cup
And he always has good luck.

James O'Connor (11)
Painsley Catholic College

A Better Place

If I could help the world,
I would rule the towns of Rome,
Dance with the people of Portugal,
And send the army back home.

I would bring world peace to everyone,
Give homes and food to the poor,
I would throw climate change into the bin,
And give it to the planet next door.

Animals would be safe and free,
All of them would stand tall,
Children of the world would play together,
As God would hug them all.

Everyone would always be happy,
Harmony would be unfurled,
The world would be a better place,
Oh! What a wonderful world!

Bethany Pearson (12)
Painsley Catholic College

Homeless

From all around me seeps the rain,
The roof, the door, my clothes, the drain,
I try to organise my bed,
It's all so soaked, I walk instead.

The comforts people take for granted,
Are the only things I wanted,
A warm, dry house, a decent meal,
Are things I crave to have, to feel.

The hours still pass, the sun still sets,
I'm walking on to hide from debts,
I crouch beneath some dingy stairs,
Tears and pain, but then, who cares?

Jacob Lovatt (12)
Painsley Catholic College

I Am The Future!

I am 'something' that no man can describe,
I have no face and no hair,
I'm not even alive!
I make the decisions,
What happens and when,
I learn to discover new things,
About humans and creatures' wings,
I can change evolution,
To unsolved solutions!
'Will the world be colourful and new?'
Says he;
'Will we be driving mini aeroplanes?'
And;
'Will the world become black and polluted, too dark for us to see?'
I'm laughing to myself,
As they are giving me all these ideas,
The dark, dark nights are drawing near.
Then I can wake up in the morning,
Bringing the happiness and tears,
You'll just have to wait and see!
The future decides . . .

Olivia Edge (12)
Painsley Catholic College

I Wish

I wish I could climb to the sky
So very, very, very high,
I wish I could climb to the moon
I hope that day will come so soon
I wish I could just fly away
And join the birds on Saturday
I wish the fish could sing to me
And for all the world to see
I wish the countries could get along
And make a family sing song.

Callum Downie (12)
Painsley Catholic College

My Hillbilly Generation

I'm a Hillbilly man
With a Hillbilly wife,
I've got 20 little kids which I threaten with my knife.
I haven't got a job,
Or even any food,
I want to be a lawyer just like Judge Jude.
All my life I've been a failure,
I just hope my kids don't follow my behaviour.
I wish I could afford a shaver - to get rid of my wife's hair,
You'd need a saviour.
My kids need food,
We need some rags,
At the moment we're wearing carrier bags.
Hear my cry, please hear my plead,
I want to learn, I want to read.
We're becoming a disfunctional nation,
Talkin' 'bout my generation.

Joseph Cooper (12)
Painsley Catholic College

Poem Of Global Warming

Come on old England, do what's right!
Come on old England, make your lives bright!
England could be such a lovely sight!
Please go green put up a fight!

We are losing animals by the minute!
The only thing that is in it . . .
Is global warming taking effect!
Come do what's right help us all!

People are helping to go green!
So please join in don't be mean
Just to begin you . . .
Start by using your recycling bin!

Aaron Eyre (11)
Painsley Catholic College

Talkin' 'Bout My Generation

Here I am in my bedroom chamber
With a model of Jesus in His manger
There is one leader, one dominant figure,
That is me of course I am the leader.

The people look up to me I am their idol
But some of them are just suicidal,
They don't like my ways and my means,
Nor do they like my brilliant schemes.

My friends are behind me, they're all I've got
But some of them jumped out the car
Shouting, 'Republic! Republic!'
They think I'm cooking something nasty in my pot!

The world is my oyster
Or so I'm told.

I go down into the street
To talk to my people,
But they just throw fruit and bags of peat
From the church steeple.

I wake up in a cold sweat
I'm 13 years old not 43
I look out my window, there's the big tree.

But I still hear the voices of the angry mob,
I see now I was an evil slob
I swore on that day I would not be a monster.

But 30 years on, I'm in my bedroom chamber
With a model of Jesus in His manger
Back then it must have been déjà vu.

Matt Spooner (13)
Painsley Catholic College

My Generation

So far in my life,
I've had many experiences,
So far in my life,
I've had happy and sad moments,
So far in my life,
I have achieved many things.

I hope that in my life,
I have a big celebration,
I hope that in my life,
I achieve one of my most wanted goals,
I hope that in my life,
I chose to be sensible.

I have experienced in my life,
Fun and laughter with friends and family,
I have experienced in my life,
Arguments and fighting with friends and family,
I have experienced in my life,
Mostly good things.

In the future I wish to
Complete something amazing!
In the future I wish to
Have a good career.
In the future I wish to,
Do what I mostly love . . . swimming.

India Cotton (12)
Painsley Catholic College

World Of Hate And Love

Bombs crashing everywhere
Smoke and gas all in the air
Dying people all around
Banging and crying are the only sounds.

Wars happening all over the world,
Everyone dying, boys and girls,
Murder, rape, bombing and kill,
Never-ending sound of the safety drill.

Women, men, boys and girls have all turned mean,
No one's safe not even the Queen
However life is not just always bad,
Having fun both girls and lads,
Love and laughter, joy and fun,
No war, no death and only toy guns.

Families being kind to each other
With a mum and dad, sisters or brothers,
No one ever mean and lie
No one ever would even try,
Because they want the world to be a happy place,
No lies, no cheats and no care for race.

The future that lies ahead of you
Make it happy whether you win or lose,
No one knows what it will be like,
Except for God up in the sky.

Sally-Ann Dunn (12)
Painsley Catholic College

Through The Eyes Of A Cat

My name's Alfie, I've got ginger fur
I'm two years old and I love to purr
I live at number eighty-four
The bad thing is - two dogs next door
Well one's OK, she's black and fluffy,
The other's nasty, brown and scruffy.

My mam's called Jude she does her best
To feed me the food I like to digest
My favourite food is fresh wild mouse
But Mam can't stand them in the house
And so at night I sneak out of my door
To catch and eat a mouse or four!

When I'm done I go back to my house
I sneak upstairs, quiet as a mouse.
I check to see who's in their bed,
Jump up, snuggle down and rest my head
The bed's so comfy, sheets like silk,
I dream of breakfast - creamy milk.

So here I am
Happy as can be
Living a life
Of luxury.

Ashleigh Humphrey (12)
Painsley Catholic College

My Life

My life is good
But I know
To make it better
There'd be snow
Lots of games
For me to buy
If there was no telly
I'd have to cry.
When I grow up
I want to be rich
Not drive my car into a ditch
So I'll work hard
And help my mum
So I'll be cool
And not be dumb.

Sullivan Edwards (11)
Painsley Catholic College

The Dragon

Do I have a meaning?
Do I have a destiny
Or will I just burn down villages?
I want to be good,
I want to help,
But every time I try to help,
They try to slay me,
So I burn their villages in anger,
I'm a dragon what do I expect,
Do I have a meaning for living? Is what I thought
But now I realise it's what you do with
The gifts in life that determines who you are.

Christopher Bullock (12)
Painsley Catholic College

My Future Poem

I wonder what my future holds
Is it fuzzy or is it bold?
I want a job that pays well
I will study hard and only time will tell
I used to think I'd fly a plane
Or maybe see what life is like in Spain
A writer, a teacher,
Or even a preacher.
I wonder if I will be rich
Or spend life in a ditch.
I will have to leave some dreams behind
But I need a job that means being kind
I hope I do my exams well
Only time will tell.

Bethany Godwin (13)
Painsley Catholic College

Harmony

In my generation I hope to see
The whole world in perfect harmony.
Like a big huge finished puzzle
And we can now take off our muzzle.

The skies would always be blue
And there'd be nothing we can't do
All the grass would be green
And no one would be mean.

If only we could all get along
And all together sing a song
Like the birds in the tree
There'd be nothing we couldn't see.

If only there were harmony.

Robin Khadjenouri (14)
Painsley Catholic College

My Future

The future will be war,
The future will be gone,
Our societies will be poor
Face the future, we have decided our doom.

Not far from now
I reckon the bombs will go boom
The war will bring cold
And before it has ended, our children will be old.

Nothing will live on,
No animals or plants
Yes, everything will be gone.

The countries will be gone, Russia, Spain and France,
I'll give you a bet
It won't happen just yet!

Matthew Priddey (14)
Painsley Catholic College

Environment We Live In!

The birds will walk
Parrots won't talk
People will fly
As time passes by
Schools won't exist
Streets full of mist
Animals are dying
People can't stop crying
Love turned to hate
No one has a mate
Everything is old
Streets are cold
Empty are beds
And my world is now dead.

Lucinda Caton-Tanner (13)
Painsley Catholic College

The Future Is Wild

Computers which do everything
Where the world's leaders do anything
All they do is sit and wait
Wait for something major to happen,
But nothing major happens.

No need to be scared
Only it bare impaired
No need for locks
Legal is everything.

If you have anything you click
No need to take the mick
Everything is peaceful
The future is wild.

Jack Pearson (13)
Painsley Catholic College

My Generation

My generation
What will it bring?
Perhaps a world without complication,
Where the grass is green,
And the skies are blue,
And all the goodness can be seen,
Where harmony and happiness is spread
By happy souls and hearts,
And everything that is said,
Is happy and special,
My generation,
My generation,
Oh what will it bring.

Sophie Bullock (13)
Painsley Catholic College

My Future Is Famous

I wasn't born to money
I wasn't born to fame
Back then when I looked to the future,
I didn't think they'd be screaming my name.
The choices I took for the future,
Were stupid but worth the risk,
But when I looked to the future, I didn't expect this.
Back then I killed my time,
Wandering quite far,
But back then when I looked to the future,
And didn't know I could make my millions with just my cheap guitar.
Back then when I was just a child
I didn't have a name,
Just mosher, goth or emo
But now it's not the same,
Because now when I walk down the street,
My name is all they say.
Too bad they can't get close enough
My bodyguards keep them away!

Hazel Cross (13)
Painsley Catholic College

In The Future

In the future the days will be bright
In the future the moon will guard the night
In the future the grass will be green
In the future less transport will be seen
In the future the birds will be singing
In the future church bells will be ringing
In the future children will be playing
In the future hooray they'll be saying
In the future bad things will be banned
In the future peace will spread over the land.

Courtney Smith (14)
Painsley Catholic College

A Whale's Side Of The Story

I am a whale, a whale whose name is Curt
And very inconveniently my feelings got hurt.

I live in the ocean and I have lots and lots of friends,
I happen to have so many that
I count them in the tens.

There came 20 friendly people
Although at first I couldn't see that they were 20
Poacher people coming to kill me.

I knew that they weren't nice
When they threw their nets into the sea
I decided as soon as I saw that
Really I must flee.

I swam away so quickly that I managed to escape.
But who knows maybe next time the poachers
Might bring mates.

Gabrielle Byrne (12)
Painsley Catholic College

My Future

As we look forward to the future,
We should remember what we are doing now,
All the jobs we do,
Like working in a zoo.

As we look forward to the future,
We should remember what we are doing now
All the home to where we belong,
Or even bein' eaten by King Kong.

As we look forward to the future,
We should remember what we are doing now,
As we are only in our lower teens,
That is what not to think about.

Jacob Perks (13)
Painsley Catholic College

The Furniture

As the clock ticked away,
In the world there was no play,
When all were asleep,
The sound of music was discreet
As the chair just woke up,
The fire decided to stoke up,
As the clock constantly ticked,
The fire still flicked,
The furniture was alive,
It was literally like a beehive
The buzzing was soft,
Up in the loft,
The furniture with the moth-eaten sheets,
Came to life within three feet,
Up there,
There is no mayor,
But just the old furniture,
That has no use.

Jack Bourne (13)
Painsley Catholic College

Through The Eyes Of Cheeky

Cheeky is my name
I never put them to shame
I love everybody and they love me too
When they come up to me I just say boo
To you!

When people ride me I do what they say
I never buck them off
I am a right big mouth.

I love Cheeky Chops
That is his name
I don't care I love them all the same.

Lucy Chadwick (12)
Painsley Catholic College

Through A Dancer's Eyes

Tonight's the night
Here I go,
I feel happy and full of might
Going backstage,
Waiting for my turn,
It's like opening a new page,
Here we all go floating like kites,
Leaping and twirling,
Feeling the heat from the lights,
It's now the end,
Disappointment fills the air,
I say goodbye to a great weekend.

Lucy Goodwin (12)
Painsley Catholic College

Our World

Earth is a planet under the sun
A planet made of miracles
Full of love and hope
Just as God wanted it to be.

But there's us on this planet
We cause war and poverty
We bring destruction and death
But we also save and preserve
This beautiful world.

This is our world.

Philippa Oakden (13)
Painsley Catholic College

In The Future

In the future:
There will be wars and death,
Many new diseases and many
New cures,
Bombs will be dropped,
People will die and people will cry.

The technology will be so cool
Slavery will be so common and
Racism will only get worse.
The Queen will have changed
And life could go from good
To bad in a flash.

In the future anything could
Happen.

Jessica Greensmith (12)
Painsley Catholic College

What The Future Brings

I am a person with many dreams
My life may not be as it seems
Is my future grey, is it bright
Will it sink down, will it take flight?
What will the future hold for me?
Will it make me as busy as a bee?
Now I am lonely and no one cares
I wonder if my future is anything like theirs.
Will my life be a life worth living?
After all I haven't been giving
I sleep under the stars when it is sunny
I am a tramp I have no money.

Isobel Alkins (12)
Painsley Catholic College

Through An Old Lady's Eyes

I am an old woman now
Looking on my past
Thinking about the good old times
Oh my they've flown so fast.

Let me tell you a little story
About when I was a girl
Me and my sis
Would run away
To a place quite like this
We would stay there for hours
Watching the birds
As they flew away and sang.

I am an old woman now
Looking on my past
Thinking about the good old times
Oh my they've flown so fast.

Georgia Bennett (12)
Painsley Catholic College

My Generation

In my generation there are lots of us,
We all catch up on the latest buzz,
Either playing games,
Or calling each other names,
Trying to get the latest technology,
But some of us care about biology,
Most of us are bored of school,
I'd rather be playing in a swimming pool,
As we go through adolescence,
We all start to lose our sense,
As we start now to grow,
Sometimes we feel very low.

Connor Forrester (12)
Painsley Catholic College

In My Days . . .

In my days
There were scooters,
Now there's petrol scooters.

In my days
People played board games
Now they play computer games.

In my days
I had to help around
Now people are lazy.

In my days
It was much better
But now it's changed
That was my generation.

Hannah Griffin (12)
Painsley Catholic College

My Generation

My generation
Eco-friendly life, computer
Gaming and friends.

My generation
Outdoor activities, fresh air
And exercise.

My generation
Watching the TV soaps and
Music, couch potatoes.

My generation
Going green, protect our
Own environment, please.

Kieran Barron (12)
Painsley Catholic College

Our World, The Wonderful World

The world is wonderful,
The creation of God,
Filled with humans and the animals that surround us.
The smell of the flowers are sweet,
And as the wind blows the leaves fall off the trees.
I love God's creation,
It is fantastic,
Even when I am feeling down,
I wonder how He did this creation,
It must have took a long time.

Stacey Osborne (12)
Painsley Catholic College

School Plays

'Romeo and Juliet' is so boring
All I do is end up snoring.

'Snow Queen' is so mean
I bet her room isn't clean.

I bet 'Hamlet' said
I'm not going to bed.

If 'Macbeth' didn't die
He would have suffered Nan's pie.

'Oliver' deserves the best
My nan would make him a vest.

'Joseph' had weird dreams
While eating custard creams.

Dorothy had red shoes
I wonder if she met Tom Cruise.

Calum Stratton (12)
Ryecroft CE Middle School

A2Z Of Modern Life

All around there is a beat
Beat box on da street
Chillin' is da law
Destroying da front door
Eggin' people's houses
Flippin' people are louses
Gangs with their guns
Hip hop in da slums
I is as cool as an ice cube
JK is da king of da chube
Kickin' your 'ed in
Laugh at the bloke in da bin
Metallica is da band
New lad in da land
'Ole in me 'ed but I ain't dead
Person who shot said
Queen is da gang'
Wit all your twang
Yo yo yo let's go
Zang all the twang yo.

Dan Lear (12)
Ryecroft CE Middle School

If My Dog Sam Could Talk

If my dog Sam could talk he'd say:

I have one brown ear and the rest of me is white
Jack's my master, he praises me,
Smiles, strokes and fusses me.
I have his pants at night when he changes for bed.
I would sleep on his bed if he had a low bed.
I am unique,
I am a mongrel of many mongrels.
I smell when I'm wet.
My thick black lips sometimes make a big smile.
I am Sam.

Jack Martin (11)
Ryecroft CE Middle School

2007s Girls

2007s girls always . . .

Worry about their looks
Taking their mirrors everywhere

Text on their mobiles
Usin' slang wordz

Go out to long night discos
Then late for school the next day

Flirt with their boyfriends
Later being dumped

Eat too much junk food
Then next trying to burn it off

Go shopping every day
With lots of money to spend

I love being a girl
And I don't know who wouldn't.

Emma Addison (11)
Ryecroft CE Middle School

Lessons

Boring lessons, snoring lessons
Confusing lessons, amusing lessons,
Lessons that can take all day
When kids like us could go and play
Eating, making, bad lessons
Meeting, creating, mad lessons!
Drawing lessons, cooking lessons
Could go horribly wrong lessons
Science lessons, reading lessons
Geography and IT lessons.

Teachers are obsessed with lessons
Me, I hate 'em, I'm confessing!

Reuben Wilson (11)
Ryecroft CE Middle School

Ten Things You Might Find In The Batmobile!

A tracking device that will hunt you down,
A labelled picture of the evil clown.
A poster of Batgirl doing a pose,
Snot all over it from Batman's nose.
Tons of bats,
With their favourite meal, rats.
A miniature grapple gun,
Dartboard in the back for having fun.
A bat shaped mobile phone,
A half eaten ice cream cone.
A massive widescreen TV,
Next to it a jar of Earl Grey tea.
The Batmobile is completely packed,
You can't come soon the bat's been sacked.

Tristan Marsh (12)
Ryecroft CE Middle School

What I'm Made Of

Me, I'm not your
Innocent little sweetie.
I'm little Miss Rude.
Go away if I told you to!
I'll get mad if you don't listen to me.
Football's what I live for,
Getting dirty is my aim.
Not doing as I'm told gets me
On top!
Anyway why do you care?
Well I say you've got to read it all
So do that.
Hey I'm not your little Miss
I'm your tall girl.
So I'm too tall for all of you!

Kelly Walker (11)
Ryecroft CE Middle School

What I Learnt At School Today

At school I've learnt a lot of things,
I really like to do,
Like running down the hallway
And eating blobs of glue.

I love to hum and chew my gum,
I've practised you can tell,
With a pencil dangling out my nose,
I look like something from Hell.

English, maths, science, French,
Either too hard or just a bad stench,
Don't even ask about history,
I just find that a complete mystery.

Even though I find it boring,
And sometimes find myself snoring,
Overall it's actually good,
Especially the yummy school pud!

Jasmin Martin (11)
Ryecroft CE Middle School

What's In A Teacher's Drawer

Nobody knows what's in a teacher's drawer.
They say if you go in there you have broken the law.

So one day we all dared to go in,
The contents was like the school's dustbin.

There was a half eaten fruit nut bar,
The rusty rotten keys from her old red car,
A mouldy sandwich that was there last week,
And a toy mouse that went *squeak, squeak,*
A bottle of perfume that I fainted by the smell
Then we heard that dreaded bell.

So now you know what's in a teacher's drawer,
So remember it really is breaking the law.

Fern Adams (12)
Ryecroft CE Middle School

Dogs In Every Different Type!

Dogs for me
Dogs for you
Even dogs on the loo.

Pretty dogs
Butch dogs
Even eating your lunch dogs.

Big dogs
Little dogs
Having a little jig dogs.

Rough dogs
Fluffy dogs
Even extremely tough dogs.

Calm dogs
Crazy dogs
Black and white farm dogs.

Thin dogs
Fat dogs
Rummage through the bin dogs.

Dogs are not just for Christmas
They are for your life

So take care of them
Like they are your husband or wife!

Sophie Robotham (11)
Ryecroft CE Middle School

Songs!

Sad songs,
Happy songs,
Dancing about songs.

Jazz songs,
Pop songs,
And just plain bad songs.

Long songs,
Short songs,
Are they ever gonna end songs.

Girls' songs,
Boys' songs,
Mix and match songs.

Old songs,
New songs,
Never will forget songs.

Slow songs,
Fast songs,
Tires you out songs.

Loved songs,
Hated songs,
Can't handle them, songs.

My songs,
Your songs,
Everybody's favourite songs!

Georgina Stokes (12)
Ryecroft CE Middle School

Things You Would Find
In Your Dad's Bathroom

A rubber ducky ready to be squeezed,
A nose trimmer with a flat battery,
Even conditioner that my dad didn't need,
A bottle of shampoo that ran out last week,
A cracked tap which sprays you in the face,
As well as the toilet that had a leak,
A mouldy bar of soap,
A pair of last month's socks,
And a toothbrush which hangs on a rope,
A towel used when Dad comes home from work,
When Dad sings in the shower it's worse than a growl,
A cracked mirror seven years bad luck,
A window which is always open,
And then on top of the toilet Dad's lorry book,
My dad's shower cap from the 80s,
A wet toilet seat from when the rain comes in,
But he tells me don't forget to wash your shouldeez,
There is a ripped shower curtain,
A broken doorknob,
But most of all we say it is an awful room, that's for certain!

Ben Clowes (11)
Ryecroft CE Middle School

Things I'd Do If It Wasn't For Mum

Things I'd do if it wasn't for Mum:

Things would be much better than now,
I'd go to bed just when I want, and make my brothers say ow,
I wouldn't have to do my homework, or ask before I go out,
I'd never have to be quiet; I would just shout and shout and shout,
I would not go to school, because I'd always be at my friends,
And I'd constantly be reading mags to find the latest trends,
I could go and buy whatever I want, and never do another sum,
But who would cook my meals? I suppose I need my mum!

Rebecca Ward (11)
Ryecroft CE Middle School

The Big Blast!

Computerised gizmos . . . everyone's dream
Latest gadgets in a steady stream
Remote controls in living rooms
Guzzling engines, billowing fumes
Supersonic travel has come our way
Everything is there to be thrown away.

Blast!
Just wait one minute
Last chance - desperate - save the planet
Left it till the 11th hour
Reuse, recycle, wind and solar power
Your carbon footprint, reduce CO_2 emission
That's got to be our global mission.

If we learn from the present and reflect from the past
We can reshape the future and avoid a big *blast!*

Harley Bussey (11)
Ryecroft CE Middle School

Things You Will Find In A Teacher's Drawer!

A half eaten apple core all gone rotten,
A load of textbooks all been forgotten
A mobile phone with unread texts,
A big long receipt for clothes from Next
A large supply of Pepsi to keep her going,
An old tennis ball that used to be good for throwing
An old CD back from the 80s
A scruffy piece of work that used to be Katie's
A snotty tissue all slimy and green,
The most embarrassing knickers you've ever seen!

Polly Clowes (11)
Ryecroft CE Middle School

What Am I Made Of?

I don't wear pretty little dresses
Or stick to the rules
I am not friends with everyone
Never good as gold
I tell you what I think
Rules are for breaking
Homework is pointless
And I am made for getting mucky
I aim to keep my room untidy
I don't tuck my shirt in
Or make my tie really long
Silence isn't golden
I don't tell the truth all the time
But one thing I always do is my dares
So you watch out!

Emily Heathcote (11)
Ryecroft CE Middle School

What I Would Do If It Wasn't For My Mum

I would:

Party all night
Pick a fight
Eat cakes
Chocolate flakes
Have no school
Be a fool
Play my drums
Have sore thumbs
Make a mess
Nevertheless
Take a nap
Play some rap
Eat junk food
Be a dude.

Aaron Stones (11)
Ryecroft CE Middle School

Things I'd Do If It Wasn't For My Mum

I would
Paint my room bright red
Kick my brother in the head
Sleep in all day
Set fire to lots of hay
Stay up all night
Until I get a fright
Drive the car
Smash things with a crowbar
Skip school
Jump in a swimming pool
Hit my brother till he cries
Cover it up with a lie
Eat junk food
Be a dude
Become a millionaire
Then a billionaire.

Anthony Lane (11)
Ryecroft CE Middle School

Wonderful Animals!

Cute newts
Drunk skunks
Fab crabs
Funky monkeys
Hyper vipers
Nile crocodiles
Perky turkeys
Pretty kitties
Shy butterflies
Magical animals!
These are in the animal kingdom,
They have wit and lots of wisdom!

Kristie Beddoes (11)
Ryecroft CE Middle School

Teachers!

Kind teachers, nasty teachers,
Mix and match teachers.

Ugly teachers, pretty teachers,
Can't stand to look at them teachers.

Cool teachers, weird teachers
Absolutely freaky teachers.

Sad teachers, happy teachers,
Totally depressed teachers.

Busy teachers, lazy teachers,
Type who think they're funny teachers.

Scary teachers, silly teachers,
The same old boring teachers.

So all-in-all teachers are strange
But they're the ones that fill our brains!

Harriet Brodie (11)
Ryecroft CE Middle School

If A Baby Could Talk

If a baby could talk it would sound a little bit like this . . .

Get me a squishy thing to hold!
Granny slippers, I am cold!
Change me Dad cuz I have poohed!
Hurry up Mum I want food!
You'd better shut up or there will be a riot!
My favourite Teletubbie is on - quiet
Not football change over the channel!
Time for bed get me a warm flannel!

And get me my dummy sharpish!

Martha Baker (11)
Ryecroft CE Middle School

Mum For Sale!

My mum is for sale.
She:
Likes the chippy
Puts on lippy
Goes on walks
And watches hawks.
Does the wash
Likes her nosh
Gets up early
Is very girly.
Cleans the sinks
And hardly blinks.
Goes to sleep
When counting sheep.
She drinks tea
At half-past three.
Please take my mum
She is not dumb!

William Heathcote (11)
Ryecroft CE Middle School

Homework

Homework boring homework!
We get it every day
I can't go on the PlayStation
I can't go out to play.

Homework boring homework!
Today it's geography maps
It wrecks your weekends
I need to do my racing laps.

Homework boring homework!
What is it all about?
The teachers say it helps us,
So they must be right - no doubt!

Declan Lander (12)
Ryecroft CE Middle School

Cricket Crazy

I like playing cricket
I can take a wicket
I try to hit it hard
I'm never caught off guard
You have to hit the ball
Yes or no, you should call
When you are bowling
The ball might be rolling
If they hit it quite far
They might hit a car
In the middle of a match
You should take a good catch
If you hit a good four
You could be on a lot more.

Joe Cliffe (11)
Ryecroft CE Middle School

Holiday

Sunset, sea, sand
Open the door
And the weather
Is grand.

Swimming costume,
Sunglasses, suncream
At the ready!
Find a shady hammock,
Try and keep it steady.

Floating on a lilo
Squinting at the sky,
If only life could always be as carefree as this,
I thought with a sigh.

Eliza Ollerenshaw (12)
St Dominic's School, Brewood

Endangered

I am so endangered
I am so frightened of being extinct,
I am scared of being Man's trophy,
I am over a hundred years old,
Many of my friends have disappeared,
Off this planet,
All of my friends were here one day, and gone the next.

Endangered is not so scary,
You get used to it,
One day I'll be gone from this planet,
One day I might reappear with all my friends,
One day I will be back
If I get extinct.

Laura Tarbuck (14)
St Dominic's School, Brewood

Comparisons

Litter in the park so high,
The beach is where people lie.

While the roads twist and turn,
The harbour's boats will return.

The cars rush past the house,
The sea is as quiet as a mouse.

I lived in a town that's all,
Now I live in a village so small.

I enjoy peaceful days,
And would not swap for those city ways.

Hollie Read (11)
St Dominic's School, Brewood

Animal Antics

Sleepy, slimy, scaly slug slithers silently, sneakily down the
segmented slippery slide.
The segmented, slippery slide which the sleepy, slimy, scaly slug
slithered down, squeaked shakily.
So that sleepy, slimy, scaly slug slid down the segmented
slippery slide.

Happy, hungry hippo, haughtily heaved up a hilariously huge hill.
The hilariously huge hill which the happy, hungry hippo haughtily
heaved himself up hit hippo horribly.
So that now unhappy, hungry hippo had to heave himself down the
hilariously huge hill.

Daft, dirty, dodgy dog dragged down the dreaded den.
The dreaded den which the daft, dirty, dodgy dog dragged himself
down doomed dog dirtily.
So that doomed, daft, dirty, dodgy dog dragged himself away from
the dreaded den.

Charlotte Davies (11)
St Dominic's School, Brewood

My Family

F or we are all different!
A gree and disagree like people clashing . . .
M y mother loves me and my brother, so does my father!
   Irresponsible that's me . . . Perfect that's my brother!
   But all the same
I t's like your journey in life is a ribbon of moonlight
L oving my family is easy, you just need to be yourself
Y es we are all different but really we are all the same!

Maneshia Johal (11)
St Dominic's School, Brewood

Christmas

The turkey is stuffed; the presents are under the tree
The children are tucked up in bed awaiting Santa's delivery,
The house is lit up like a matchstick,
We're so filled up with Christmas pudding we could be sick!

The children rip open their presents, eyes beaming with delight
The garden outside is coated in white,
The fire is on, and the house is cosy!

The tree is decorated covered in light,
No one will be able to sleep on this Christmas night!
The Queen's speech is on the telly!
All the family are getting quite merry!

Molly Hyson (12)
St Dominic's School, Brewood

Homework

Another night at the kitchen table,
When all I want is to watch cable,
My favourite show is on again,
But maths, art and physics what a pain.

Now it's late need to eat my tea,
Need to spend time with my family,
I want to play with my dog, Mable,
But I'm still sitting at the kitchen table.

I'm watching the clock
Going *tick-tock*
Got to finish writing this fable
But I'm still sitting at the kitchen table!

Jordana O'Reilly (12)
St Dominic's School, Brewood

The Race!

There goes one
There goes another
There goes someone off to their mother
Hobbling along, hurt his knee,
'You were being silly, told you see!'

Trip goes her
Trip goes him
Trip goes someone who breaks a limb
He is down and upset, crying, crying,
The parents around, sighing, sighing.

Stumble goes a female
Stumble goes a male
Stumble goes someone who falls over a rail
Quickly gets up in case of a train
'And now I think you better use your brain!'

Hannah Cox (11)
St Dominic's School, Brewood

Shopping!

S hopping, shopping, spend, spend, spend
H ours of fun with my friend
O pulent handbags, purses and shoes
P arty dresses we've seen in the news
P ick what you want and hope that it fits
I nto the bag go bobs and bits
N ow we've emptied most the shops,
G irls night in to try on our tops.

Elizabeth Butler (12)
St Dominic's School, Brewood

Just A Bit Of Fun

Just a bit of fun
That's what she'd say.
Who knew one drop of vodka
Would make her feel this way.

But now it's inside her,
There's no turning back.
That tiny drop of poison,
Will turn her lungs to black.

Now all she wants is more,
It's not poison in her brain,
It's making her go crazy,
It's driving her insane.

'Just a bit of fun,'
That's what she said,
Who knew one drop of vodka
Would make her end up dead.

Demie Allport (13)
St Dominic's School, Brewood

Dream!

My dream is for people to stand up for themselves
We must say stop to war
No more children saying, 'I'm scared.'
We should all be free
Like peace
Like our lives
How we want it to be
Get those terrorists to disappear
Why should we let people risk their own lives
Just so we can be happy?

Annabel Randev (13)
St Dominic's School, Brewood

The World In Which We Live

In this age that I've been born
The whole wide world seems to be torn -
Terrorism, fighting, civil war
Abuse, divorce, breaking the law
No one seems to have a care
No one seems to have time to spare.

These are some of the bad things with which I live
Anti social behaviour, nothing seems to give.
The world is heating up, ice melting fast,
Because of all the bad things we have had in the past
So now we're trying to put our planet to rights
Global warming is always there in our sights.

Computers, iPods, mobiles too
All of this is just for you
Televisions and planes as well
All of this is just quite swell
Schools and lessons help you out
So don't give them any doubt.

The summers are warm but the winters are cold
Autumn and spring becoming quite bold
There's beautiful things upon this Earth
We've all enjoyed it for what it's worth
My generation is doing its best
But time will be the ultimate test.

Hannah Smith (13)
St Dominic's School, Brewood

My Dog Oliver

My dog Oliver
O is for obedient I don't think so
L is for love it always shows
My dog Oliver
So small but so bold.

My dog Oliver
I is for inquisitive, everyone knows
V is for valiant right down to his toes
My dog Oliver
So small but so bold.

My dog Oliver
E is for eccentric he is as mad as a fish
R is for radiant he makes me wish
My dog Oliver
So small but so bold
Always a wonder
Forever to behold.

Abigail Watkins (12)
St Dominic's School, Brewood

My Little Rabbit Starski

My little rabbit, Starski loves nothing more
Than to be tickled under the chin.
In my eyes he's a winner in everything.
His tired little eyes light up when he sees my face.
He always loves to jump to get attention.
He walks away with his tail wobbling.
He is a little softy really.
That is my little rabbit Starski.

Katherine Rigg (11)
St Dominic's School, Brewood

Life Is For Living

Life is for living
So live it to the extreme
And when new challenges come along
Make sure you're very keen.

Love yourself and hold your head high
When you feel nobody cares
As somebody will always look after you
Even when you're worse for wear.

Look on the bright side of life
When you feel down or sad
Make life a joy to live
And don't look back on what you had.

Life is for living
So live it to the extreme
And when new challenges come along,
Make sure you're very keen.

Rachel Hollingsworth (14)
St Dominic's School, Brewood

The Girl

She's got stacks and stacks of shoes
She's got a million different pairs
Piled high up in the wardrobe
Or stuffed beneath the stairs.

As she goes hunting around the High Street
She gets that label fever
She really loves the fashion scene
That cool designer diva!

She's lovely and she's gorgeous
She's mad and oh so funny
Always glad, she's never sad
An adorable hunny bunny!

Charlotte Jones (11)
St Dominic's School, Brewood

Me

I'm five feet two
So I guess I'm quite small
I've got two left feet
So I always trip up and fall.

I've got little eyelashes
And big brown eyes
A big mouth
So I'm good at telling lies.

I've got small hands
And size three feet
I probably have to look up
At everyone I meet.

I have pink cheeks
And long brown hair
And if I come across a spider
It'll give me a scare.

I talk an awful lot
And as you can see
This poem's been describing
Simple, little me.

Henrietta Painter (13)
St Dominic's School, Brewood

Please Help Me!

Why is there no one there for me?
To love me,
To care for me?
Why am I mistreated
Beat on
And unfed?
Please help me!
I need love and care.

Katie Woods (13)
St Dominic's School, Brewood

Cliques, Cliques and More Cliques

It started off with everyone the same,
But then in my time it all started to change,
The change was sweeping quickly and worldwide,
Now everyone had something to hide.
The goths stuck together and talked about stuff,
And if that even wasn't enough,
More cliques formed and you should be warned,
They came in force, got ready then swarmed.
Chavs, greebos, punks and geeks
Used to be friends and now don't like to meet.
The emos and nerds could always be heard,
Shouting and screaming every time one said a word.
They didn't get on and that was that,
Each clique treated others just like rats,
And often called each other . . . it would be better if
I didn't say that perhaps.
We're not all that different and should just get on,
Instead of sitting and waiting like a time bomb,
And then the world will all be gone,
And it's a shame if we're to end with no one getting on.

Charlotte Grainger (12)
St Dominic's School, Brewood

Glamorous!

My room is the nicest you will ever see
I don't believe in being a busy bee.

Instead I like to lie around
Not even making a single sound.

I'll put on my new face
And leave the house without a trace.

I'll go fetch my card
And then shop extremely hard.

And when I have decided to come on home
I'll chill out in the chilling zone.

Georgina Wood (12)
St Dominic's School, Brewood

Sticking To My Generation

This generation is a gadget phase,
Not like the olden days,
Phones, iPods, MSN,
Now people know of all of them,
Beeping tractors for little boys,
All these new modern toys,
Global warming for a start,
But moving onto a better part,
From a simple lolly on a stick,
To one that comes with sherbet dip,
None of the grown-ups can keep up,
The olden days with them has stuck,
From the simple horse and carriage,
To a lovely modern garage,
Maybe it's me, who can't keep up,
But one thing I know,
With this generation, I have stuck.

Hannah Bowen (12)
St Dominic's School, Brewood

Save Our World!

Global warming isn't hard to explain
It's how all humans damage their domain
It hurts the planet more every day
It's essential we act without delay.

Recycle your bottles, papers and tins
And try to put fewer things in your bins
Reduce central heating a few degrees
And help to reduce the level of seas.

Switch off completely - don't leave on standby
And make our planet less likely to die
Time is running out, we mustn't be slow
Stand up to the challenge, let's do it, let's go!

Salma Nadim (12)
St Dominic's School, Brewood

My Generation

Thinking, wondering, fearing the future,
Decisions, decisions,
Learning, living, hoping.

The people around me are never the same,
Goths, emos, all that's just a mask to hide their emotions,
People think 'I must fit in!'
But fit in with what?

As each year passes new things are made,
New opportunities arise.
Satellites, mobiles, laptops, iPods, video games,
With each new idea comes the thought
Will it work?

Like a satellite in space it is up to us
If we explode on the launch pad,
Or make it to the stars!

The world around us is dying every day,
Sadly and slowly plunging into darkness.
The evil, the hate, the hurt, and the sorrow.
The continuous controversy over life and death.

God's world, the people's world, our world.
No matter how much we try, we can never conquer the miracle of life.

Thinking, wondering, fearing the future.
Decisions, decisions,
Learning, living, hoping.

Jessica Mackriel (12)
St Dominic's School, Brewood

e-Me . . . The Electronic-Me In The Twenty First Century . . .

Everything's about change
It's all a different range
Different since 1962
That's including me and you
It's all about e-Me
In the twenty first century . . .

Technology that's a story
Everything's a possibility
Xbox 360 and Nintendo Wii
You can use them both on your TV
It's all about e-Me
In the twenty first century . . .

Now music-wise
You'd be surprised
Forget about your piano
Get yourself an iPod Nano
It's all about e-Me
In the twenty first century . . .

Orange, T-Mobile, Vodafone
There is never a need to be on your own
The cable is here with MTV
It's the end of terrestrial TV
It's all about e-Me
In the twenty first century . . .

Email, YouTube, MSN
I don't know who invented them
Everything is watched on CCTV
I'm going home to log on to my PC
It's all about e-Me
In the twenty first century . . .

Aoife Richardson (12)
St Dominic's School, Brewood

My Stereotypical Generation

Walk into the town
We're looking around
Is something you are forced to do.
The trends hit you like a bullet,
The town is split like the Red Sea.
Groups of hoodies, staring at the floor,
You look down in case the ground has
Become anything special.

Gangs, graffiti, grebos,
Bring a holocaust of chaos
Interrupting the silent floor watching
iPods, mp3s turn on and suddenly the
Town becomes a giant speaker playing
Millions of different tracks.

Chavs sitting on the railings
Goths sitting on the steps
Making the steps unusable
This is what I see
This is my stereotypical generation.

Lydia Dyer (12)
St Dominic's School, Brewood

My Poem About School

School work is tough
I've really had enough

Why oh why can't I understand
And why do I still count on my hands?

How do the teachers know so much?
I wish I had their special touch.

Chloë Sharifi (12)
St Dominic's School, Brewood

Best Friends At The Park

Best friends we are,
That's great so far,
We go to the park,
And hear the dogs bark,
We play on the swings,
And see scary things,
We play on the slides,
Wand roll on our sides,
We play in the sand,
And draw our hand,
We play in the pool,
And the lifeguard sits on a stool,
Now it's time to go for tea,
And that's the end of you and me!

Emily Loveitt (11)
St Dominic's School, Brewood

My Pets!

The black and white one with white socks on.
The ginger and white one with a moustache.
The black and white one with soft fur.
The ginger and white one with fluffy fur.
Two cats nearly alike
Both boys
      Sooty and Teddy
         They
            Are so cute!

Poppy Benkwitz (12)
St Dominic's School, Brewood

Size OO

Thin, fat, slim, tall?
Should I be on the catwalk at all?
Do I look thin? Is my bum big?
Do my bones stick out of my skin?
I'm scarily shallow,
I'm pale and thin.
Do I eat? No, I daren't.
I must spit out, the calories count.
My head's so fuzzy, I cannot count,
My memory's trashed, it's so burnt out.
Is it pretty? Does it hurt?
Deep inside it's just like Hell.

Ellie Durnall (14)
St Dominic's School, Brewood

Dreaming

I close my eyes and I'm in America
Going on all the rides in Florida,
And swimming with dolphins.

I'm walking down the high streets,
In New York, buying designer clothes
I'm sunbathing on a beautiful beach,
Then suddenly I wake up.

I realise I am dreaming,
And hope that it will come true,
One day.

Hannah Sefton (13)
St Dominic's School, Brewood

Norman Gnome

He lives in the garden, looking good
Just like a garden gnome should.
All day long he busies himself
Just like a dutiful gnomey elf.

He likes the sun, he likes the rain
You never hear Norman gnome complain.
Fishing all day with his rod and line
Perched on a rock by the *no fishing* sign.

He guards the garden from nasty prey
Cats and dogs, they run away.
'Alkazam, Alakazoo'
Norman gnome puts a spell on you.

So take heed and be aware
When Norman gnome gives you a stare.
He could be thinking up a spell
Which may not leave you feeling well.

Philip Hallworth (12)
St Thomas More Catholic College, Stoke-on-Trent

Dance Of The Snowflakes

In act 1 of the Nutcracker,
It ends with a stunning scene,
Set in the land of snow,
Where all the snowflakes dance a dream.

They sweep onto the stage,
Dressed in sparkling costumes,
They float and twirl,
Just like a flurry of soft snowflakes!

Glittering in the moonlight,
They drift among the trees,
Silhouetted against the sky,
It is a silent night.

Ann Johnson (12)
St Thomas More Catholic College, Stoke-on-Trent

Witnessing Fireworks

Rockets,
Rainbows, exploding in the sky,
Shooting away from the fuses
On which they were tied.

Sparklers
Glowing,
Yellow rays,
Fizzing, bright,
Making everyone's days.

Catherine wheels' colours,
The squealing sound,
Lighting up people's faces,
As bright sparks hit the ground.

Roman candle fountains,
In the dark night,
Shoot masses of brightness
And bring colourful light.

Airbomb Repeaters
Having a very cool name,
And the rockets like stars
In the sky, set the sky aflame.

Susannah Owen (12)
St Thomas More Catholic College, Stoke-on-Trent

My Poem

I am running out of time,
To write this silly poem.
The clock is ticking madly,
But it just seems to be flowing.

When I sit down at my desk,
And wonder what to write.
I think and think and think
All through the night.

Jack Twigg (12)
St Thomas More Catholic College, Stoke-on-Trent

Fireworks

Rockets whizzing,
Illuminate the night
An explosion of colour
A beautiful sight.

Roman candle
Crackling fountain
Sparks jump high
As high as a mountain.

Catherine wheels spin
Like a ball of fire
Each flame jumps
Higher and higher

Traffic lights glow
Red, yellow, green
The most beautiful sight
Ever to be seen.

Sparklers glitter
Red and gold
A colour explosion
Vivid and bold.

Catherine Hawley (12)
St Thomas More Catholic College, Stoke-on-Trent

Flowers!

A red little bud going to be a rose,
Everybody watching, watching how it grows!

Bluebells beaming, beaming in the grass,
Everyone smiling, smiling as they pass.

Pink little poppies shining in the sun,
With little children playing, having lots of fun.

Holly Marie Dunn (11)
St Thomas More Catholic College, Stoke-on-Trent

Wonders Of Fireworks

A torch of hope in a world of darkness,
The sparkler's crackling cry!
Its exuberance is a small child's wish
That goes out with a sigh.

The spinning cogs called
Catherine wheels light up the darkest corner
Bringing hope to everyone
The very last mourner.

The rockets zoom
The rockets dance
Seeing one is a fast gone chance
Their work done,
They fall down to Earth
Then extinguish with a sigh.

Years come, then go again
I always remember the 5th of November!

Flora Byatt (12)
St Thomas More Catholic College, Stoke-on-Trent

Fireworks!

Bang! There goes another one,
Screaming as it goes.
It's getting high
Up in the sky
And fizzle - there she blows!

Whoosh! Up high above the house,
Behind a trail of sparks.
Yellow, orange,
Red and white,
Exploding in the dark!

Hannah Rickard (11)
St Thomas More Catholic College, Stoke-on-Trent

Fireworks

Fireworks flit,
Fireworks fly,
Whizzing fast
Through the sky.

Up they go
At the speed of light
Flying graciously like a kite.

Then down they come
Spinning from above
Fluorescent lights
Fizzing loudly
Making us warm inside
They should feel so much pride.

Keira Taylor (12)
St Thomas More Catholic College, Stoke-on-Trent

Fireworks

Hissing up at high speed,
That pop upon the night.
Fall back down in great need
Many colours of blue, yellow and white.

Great big bang that is loud,
Creates a great atmosphere
Looking over people with proud
Blending in with the clouds.

Catherine wheels spin around,
With many colours that are seen.
They stop whirling and make a sound,
And what a wonderful scene.

Matthew Gordon (12)
St Thomas More Catholic College, Stoke-on-Trent

Cute Kittens

K ittens are cute, lovable and sweet,
I n the garden they'll play and do tricks for a treat!
T hey jump on your lap looking for a hug,
T hey'll play with a ball of wool under the rug.
E ach one is soft and furry too,
N on-stop they'll play and only wear out you!
S ome like to play more than others.

A nd some will sleep under your bedcovers
R eally I should warn you don't pull their tail
E ven though they may rip up your mail.

C ool cats have a really great name,
U nlikely are you to find two the same
T una they will eat, so I'd hide it if I were you
E ven though some people say they're not cute,
                          you know what's really true.

Savannah Fradley (12)
St Thomas More Catholic College, Stoke-on-Trent

On Hallowe'en Night

On Hallowe'en night all the ghouls come out to play,
They come out at dark not bright in the day.
On Hallowe'en night all zombies come out of the graves,
And the dangerous bats come out from the caves.

On Hallowe'en night witches fly high up in the sky,
They will scare and terrify all passers-by.
On Hallowe'en night all you can hear are screams,
From all the witches who gang up in teams.

On Hallowe'en night no child can sleep,
They think monsters will arise from the deep.
On Hallowe'en night at the end of it all,
All witches, monsters and ghosts have a grand ball.

Helena Wegierak (12)
St Thomas More Catholic College, Stoke-on-Trent

A Bad Day At School

Today I had my first bad day in school
The teacher started screaming at me
Just for pushing somebody in the pool
It wasn't even that serious.

The boy just drowned for a couple of minutes
The teacher jumped in and got him
With her face as red as a raspberry
She started screaming, 'What have you done, Tim?'

They had to call my parents in
Just to tell them what I'd done
And then in PE I got put in the sin bin
Just for a minor foul.

This was the worst day for me in school
But it was just going to get worse when I got home
With my parents screaming at me,
'How can you push someone in a pool?'

Junaid Ishfaq (11)
St Thomas More Catholic College, Stoke-on-Trent

Butterflies

Their brightly coloured wings
Shimmer in the bright sunlight.
We watch them flutter to a great height
Until they are no longer in sight!

Butterflies on a summer breeze
Dancing with the birds and the honeybees.

Amongst the flower heads they rest
Wings open so they look their best.
Peacocks, Admirals and Cabbage Whites
What a beautiful sight
All of them dancing and enjoying the sunshine bright!

Kayleigh Cooper (11)
St Thomas More Catholic College, Stoke-on-Trent

It's Got To Be Sweets

*I*t's got to be sweets
*T*hey're soo good
*S*our, chewy, crunchy, so good.

*G*otta eat sweets
y*O*u know
   *T*hey are best!

*T*asty
*O*r sweet

*B*uy some
*E*verything about them is good!

*S*weets
s*W*eets
sw*E*ets
swe*E*ts
swee*T*s
so   it'*S* got to be sweets.

Luke Critchlow (12)
St Thomas More Catholic College, Stoke-on-Trent

The Sunset

Burning red,
Scorching orange,
Sunny yellow,
Feeling mellow.

Fading away,
Like a glittery charm,
Over the bay,
Feeling calm.

Orange glow,
Shimmering light,
Now it's gone,
Say hello to the night.

Lauren West (13)
St Thomas More Catholic College, Stoke-on-Trent

What Is It

It fights in the trees,
It destroys the ground;
It kills the homes
Of the scared.

This monster shines
Only for a split second;
And its tip
Builds flames of evil.

It only takes
Its victims at night;
That pray for peace
Only peace is not there.

Now this monster
Was sent by the Devil
The Devil of Hell;
It was sent to kill.
'Leave none alive,' said the Devil,
This monster has the most shocking name.

Storm!

Danny Boulton (11)
St Thomas More Catholic College, Stoke-on-Trent

Dancing

Dancing is about doing tricks,
Like jumping into the air
And landing into the splits.

Freeze, worm, crab and chest stand,
The hardest one out of them all
Is the one-handed handstand.

Bethany Baskeyfield (11)
St Thomas More Catholic College, Stoke-on-Trent

Fireworks

A *whizz,* a *pop,* a *bang,* a *squeal*
A writhing squirming restless eel
That spins and flicks its fiery tongue
To anyone who comes along.

A stick of light, and heat and flames
A fiery wand to make you tame
As fiery spells flip out of its top
The great explosion it soon stops.

A fire that burns just like the sun
And shoots up high and bangs upon
The silent, still and peaceful night
Giving all a shocking fright.

A burning furnace in the skies
That catches other people's eyes
The shapes and colours shooting out
Say that's what Bonfire Night's about.

An atom bomb is in the sky
And makes all watching people sigh
A trillion different colours shine
And go out promptly in a line.

Luke Boulton (13)
St Thomas More Catholic College, Stoke-on-Trent

Friendship

Sing Star round at my house,
With my friends after school,
Laughter, dancing, singing,
That's what we do, it's cool!

We're there to help each other
No matter big or small,
My friends and me we're all together,
'Cause that's what friends are for!

Amy Thomas (12)
St Thomas More Catholic College, Stoke-on-Trent

11 Years, 7 Months, This Is Me!

I'm at a new school, how big is it?
Top class, harder work, I'm trying hard to fit,
Lots of new mates and a few of old,
High school's the best, or so I've been told.
Some lessons are boring like maths and IT,
But some are good like history and PE.

Little school was OK but now it's passed,
I feel a little older, I'm growing up fast.

As I get older I'm enjoying more sport,
Cycling and swimming, but no trunks, just shorts.
I like fishing and golf,
At football I'm in goal.
At cricket I keep wicket and sometimes I bowl.
But my life's not always good you see,
My sister's a pain and she really annoys me.
My parents are ace but sometimes they moan,
But I wouldn't swap this for anything,
Because my life is my own.

William Plant (11)
St Thomas More Catholic College, Stoke-on-Trent

My Christmas

Ho, ho, ho, here Santa comes
Coming down the chimneys equals dusty bums.
Drinking his milk and eating his pie
And one carrot for Rudolph to help his lazy eye.

Santa put some prezzies under the tree
He wrote a note saying they're for me.
Stockings hanging on the fireplace
Santa has left at a speedy pace.

Santa has left and now it's Christmas Day,
Opening my presents is like a Christmas relay.
Looking out the window snow is falling,
Christmas dinner is ready and Mum is calling.

Lucy Niemczyk (12)
St Thomas More Catholic College, Stoke-on-Trent

Fantastic Fireworks!

A spinning, twisting delight
A Catherine Wheel is here tonight.
Twisting, hissing and
Spinning, banging and popping.
It's like a burning comet
Or an evil spell that makes you vomit!

The little kids look like they're holding marigolds,
But they are actually sparklers which are small and gold.
Burning, glowing and glinting things
Which fizz like a wand or a burning star.

A fire cracker is here you see,
Big and rocket like it looks to me
Bursting brightly with exciting patterns
But before it pops it sees to flatten
And when it does it's like a flower opening
With a thousand and one patterns.

A twisting and turning thing is in the sky
Colourful and bright so you can see it when it's high.
It twists, it leaps, it swirls
It fizzes, it pops, it curls,
It looks like a rocket lifting
Or a small fire glinting.

Lauren Jade Ashton (12)
St Thomas More Catholic College, Stoke-on-Trent

The Dud

I bought a rocket one day
Then I lit it and it flew away.
Up into the sky, right to the top
Instead of *bang* it went *pop!*

Connel Brownsword (11)
St Thomas More Catholic College, Stoke-on-Trent

A Pony Called Speck

As he rides on through the wood
Doing things a pony should.
Clip-clop he tramples grass
Pony big and bold as brass.

On further he goes, walking calm
Surely this pony will do no harm
His rider is small but he will be safe
If only he shows the pony his faith.

He jumps and leaps all over the place
His heart now beating at a pace.
Faster, and faster he runs through the wood
You would do it if only you could.

He clears the fence and final gate
Back to his stable he can't be late.
He knows there's a prize, winner takes all,
He may take a stumble or even a fall.

But the ribbon is blue around his neck
Everyone cheers for the pony called Speck.

Chloe Jane Lawton (11)
St Thomas More Catholic College, Stoke-on-Trent

The Creepy, Scary 31st

Hallowe'en is tonight
Filling children with fright.

Children knocking door to door
Getting sweets more and more.

Vampires, mummies, fairies too,
Spirited people shouting *boo!*

Hallowe'en's not all about trick or treating
It's also about parties and friends meeting.

The night is nearly over
Children are now waiting till the next 31st of October.

Lauren Tomkinson (11)
St Thomas More Catholic College, Stoke-on-Trent

A Winter's Dream

One night in winter
I lay down my head
I dreamed about Christmas
As I lay in my bed.

I dreamed about winter
And glistening snow
I dreamed about presents
All wrapped up in bows.

I dreamed about snowballs
And the warm firelight
I dreamed about frost
All crisp and white.

Then I woke up
From my winter's dream
I smiled as I saw
The light of the moonbeam.

Cicely Lane (11)
St Thomas More Cathol0ic College, Stoke-on-Trent

Traffic

Traffic; the annoying jams
The choking fumes
That pollute the road

Traffic; the flash of the lights
The shake of the fist
Road rage takes over

Traffic; miles and miles of glowing lights
Winding in the distance
Like a swarm of fireflies

Traffic; the black tyre marks
The tell-tale sign
Of a sad tragedy.

Thomas Johnson (12)
St Thomas More Catholic College, Stoke-on-Trent

Pets

Pets can be big,
Pets can be small,
But I don't mind,
I love them all.

Some are clean,
Some are dirty,
Some are three,
Some are thirty.

Pets are cool,
Pets are ace,
Especially dogs,
When they lick your face.

Stephanie Hughes (13)
St Thomas More Catholic College, Stoke-on-Trent

Hallowe'en

Everybody trick or treating,
Knocking on doors, saying, 'Trick or treat?'
In their costumes walking round.

The houses decorated nice,
Treats being handed out
And a trickle of money in the pot,
Pumpkins being lit.

Knock-knock, go to the door
Look with fright
They get their sweets and money
And go no more.

Jessica Bould (11)
St Thomas More Catholic College, Stoke-on-Trent

Amazing Fireworks!

Fireworks are amazing things
That fly through the sky without any wings.
Shooting up above the ground
High in the sky with lots of sound.

Catherine wheels whirling forever
They cheer you up in the cold weather.
Spinning around whilst the colours change
Hypnotised by the light, it can be very strange.

The siren noise of the rockets' cries
Their exploding flashes blind your eyes.
Shooting up rapidly in the air
It's all gone so quickly, so blink if you dare.

Children with sparklers play a game
With burning lights they write their name.
Popping and sizzling until they fade out
You'll want some more to wave about.

The fountain pours out droplets of light
Cascading flames and colours so bright.
Faces light up as they watch the show
And fixed with smiles to home they go.

Holly Rutter (12)
St Thomas More Catholic College, Stoke-on-Trent

Fireworks

Boom
Bang
Way up high!
Flying
Whizzing
High in the sky!
Multicoloured
Big and small
Now it's all over we're all saying bye!

Chloe-Ann Lythgoe (12)
St Thomas More Catholic College, Stoke-on-Trent

Dolphins

Jumping and splashing,
Swimming free.
Every dolphin's home
Is in the deep blue sea.

Bottle-nosed, Amazon and white-sided,
Are to name a few.
To watch them swim,
Is a wonderful view.

They speak to one another,
In a high-pitched sound.
They are famous for their tricks,
Like spinning around.

Jumping through hoops,
And performing in large groups,
Is also very cool.

Dolphins are caring, loving and lots of fun
Now my poem is done.

Ellise Nicholls (11)
St Thomas More Catholic College, Stoke-on-Trent

Colours

Colours in the sea,
Colours in the sky,
Colours all around us
My oh my.

Colours in my dream,
While I sleep
Colours in the day
While I play.

Colours all around us
Colours everywhere
They make you want
To stop and stare.

Hayley Plant (11)
St Thomas More Catholic College, Stoke-on-Trent

Hallowe'en

Kids put on their costumes then walk around all night,
Asking for sweets and money from anyone in sight.
Later whilst they're eating their sweets they get a sudden fright.

What's that, who's there, oh my gosh, there's someone there.
They yell and scream and run for the door,
It turns out they don't have their key anymore.

I'm telling you now there's a ghost out here
Who can we shout, no one lives near.
It'll suck out our brain and eat us alive
Or maybe it'll come after us with a knife.

We suddenly realise this cannot be true
It must be a dream, so what shall we do.
Shall we try to wake up or see how it ends,
We should wake up so we can tell our friends.

Georgia Birch (11)
St Thomas More Catholic College, Stoke-on-Trent

Hallowe'en

Frights!

There is a monster by the window,
A goblin by the door,
Sometimes I think there are ghosts on my floor.
Spiders in the kitchen,
Breeding more and more.
Outside in the open little children playing,
But they are in for a fright,
Because they don't know what they are in for tonight.

Happy Hallowe'en!

Andrew Cash (11)
St Thomas More Catholic College, Stoke-on-Trent

Hockey

On Saturday I go to hockey
It makes my legs go floppy.
I also like to skate
With my mate Jake.

I always have lots of fun
On my last match we won.
My skates are too small
But they make me look tall.

I'm missing a wheel
And my hockey laces are teal.
My hockey team is good
And my name's Connor Wood.

Connor Wood (11)
St Thomas More Catholic College, Stoke-on-Trent

Anger

White hot fury burns the soul,
Rippling waves of rage,
Consumes you in a ball of passion
And holds you like a cage.

Wrath and ire rule the mind
And don't seem like they'll let go.
Hatred rules your every move
Only anger does this bestow.

And yet, perhaps, just out of sight
There's calmness putting up a fight.
It's getting stronger, stronger still,
Until at last it rules your will!

Adam Stanway (12)
St Thomas More Catholic College, Stoke-on-Trent

This Was The Way She Made Me Blush

She would smile at me
With kindness and thought
She would always show me
Her diamond-white teeth
Like she whitened them every day.
This was a way she made me blush.

She would always laugh at my jokes
Even if some of them weren't funny -
She would always mess about with me
My old teacher nearly moved us.
This was a way she made me blush.

We would take turns to stare at each other
Hoping the other person didn't know.
Her eyes sparkled like green emerald diamonds.
This was a way she made me blush.

I asked her out,
She said yes.
I had won her
But I lost her.

She made me blush
But she made me sad!

Robert Sangwa (11)
St Thomas More Catholic College, Stoke-on-Trent

The Run

Through the desert he lurches and leaps,
From the grass he peers and peeps.
Searching his prey, he stares it down,
He is the king, he has the crown.

His eyes a golden globe of light,
He laughs coolly at its sudden fright.
Then jumps at it, his claws out,
It's just then that he hears a shout.

Retreating back to the litter tray,
In the fake grass where the children play,
He prays that the woman will go away,
Here with his prey he wants to stay!

In his prayer he has no such luck,
She is now pointing at the curtain hook.
The curtain lies in a ripped state,
And in her eyes is a look of hate.

But when he miaows in his innocent way,
She knows that all he wanted to do was play.
Catty gets away with such naughty things,
Now, he thinks, for the curtain rings!

Demi Robinshaw (11)
St Thomas More Catholic College, Stoke-on-Trent

Church

The alarm bells ring,
The voices start to sing,
The organ blows out notes,
And everyone takes off their coats.

As the mass begins,
The church bell dings and dings,
The screech of the bell appears,
To make children cover their ears.

As the prayers are read out,
No child dares to shout out,
Then suddenly the organ starts to ring
The church is filled with a longing sensation to sing and sing.

The offertory is taken,
The counting must not be mistaken,
The mass has nearly ended,
And lots of people attended.

On that Sunday morning the grudges are cleared,
The word of God has spoken through everyone's ears.

Hannah Gibson (11)
St Thomas More Catholic College, Stoke-on-Trent

Cats

Running around all day long
Sweeping in and out of the grass
Long thin tails
Screeches and wails
Beady eyes.

Pointy ears and all
So loving and caring
Could sleep all day
So soft and sweet.

After all, that's a cat!

Mia Kimberley (11)
St Thomas More Catholic College, Stoke-on-Trent

Garden Activities

Want to play outside,
Then here is your guide,
On how to play great games,
Now here are your aims.

To play on your pogo stick,
And to have a little kick
About with your football,
Up against your garden wall.

There are other things to do,
Like bounce upon your new
Trampoline which is so great,
And which isn't hard to locate.

Once the day is done,
And you can't have much fun,
Then go to bed and rest your head.

Benjamin Gibson (11)
St Thomas More Catholic College, Stoke-on-Trent

Hallowe'en

Ghosts and ghouls
Witches and fools
Sweets and treats
For you to eat
Lots of fun trying to fool your mum
With your friends having a party
And hypo kids doing karate
Hallowe'en's haunted stories
Don't eat too many sweets or you
will be poorly.

Lydia Derbyshire (11)
St Thomas More Catholic College, Stoke-on-Trent

All About English

English, English to say my ABC
To do it fast just follow me.
I try my best to follow you
But I'm to shy to speak my mind.
In my world I do my best
I wish I could be like the rest.
Every day I try and try
But I get put off by the rest.
Every day goes on and on
I still get put off every one
But I'm too shy to tell them to stop
Come on teachers make them do the lot.
I will work hard so I move up to H or M
It's a long way off for, T or S
Oh my god what about the rest?

Jessica Elikowski (12)
St Thomas More Catholic College, Stoke-on-Trent

The School Dinner Ladies

They march and drill us around the square
A horrible and nasty sight.
They are your very worst nightmare,
You'll never sleep at night.
A rough and tough commando troop
They don't like kids at all.
Your head will sag and shoulders droop
Inside that dinner hall!

At
Din-din-din-er
Din-din-din-er
Time!

Olivia Tatler (11)
St Thomas More Catholic College, Stoke-on-Trent

Rat Named Pat

Pat the rat is my name
Causing trouble is my game.
I live in a cage that puts me in a rage.

Around, around the house for food,
It all depends on my mood.
Cheese and crackers are the best
But lettuce I detest.

I am the rat Pat
And now I'm very, very fat.

Can't fit in my cage,
So now I live in a hole
With a big black mole
And we're both the colour of coal.

Aimee Birks (12)
St Thomas More Catholic College, Stoke-on-Trent

Fireworks

Catherine wheels going around and around,
Spitting flames which fall to the ground.
Screamers screaming like a little kid,
Going in circles like a pot lid.
Rockets that pop upon the night,
Which explode as high as a kite.
Sparklers spitting sparks of fire,
Going in different directions like a barbed wire.
All these colours so beautiful and bright,
They are all so dangerous, so do not light.

Charlotte Melia (12)
St Thomas More Catholic College, Stoke-on-Trent

The Fireworks Show

Crackler, bright and beautiful
It reaches into the sky
It is a wonder to behold before your eyes.

Vortex, a shooting star exploding
It brightens up the sky.
It is a wonder
That will dazzle your eyes.

Fountain, a small decorated flower
Noisy but small
Mysterious and strange
That is loved by all.

Catherine wheel, a burning wheel
So fast,
So quick,
A wheel of fire that won't last.

Banger, silent rising
Loud bang,
A song,
That nobody could have sang.

Taylor Simms (11)
St Thomas More Catholic College, Stoke-on-Trent

My Cat

My cat is greedy
You'll never guess what he did
He chased a rat in the back
And put it on his mat.

The rat escaped
And my cat chased
Until he was very tired.
Lucky rat!

Samantha Clarke (12)
St Thomas More Catholic College, Stoke-on-Trent

The Countryside

Out there it is peaceful and quiet,
Flowing with wildlife but still,
There are many rare flowers,
Somewhere out there.

Out there, fish flow through streams,
And birds up in the trees,
Insects under the ground
Somewhere out there.

Out there flowers grow freely
Nothing to trample them,
Nothing to eat them
Somewhere out there.

Out there insects roam freely
Nothing to eat them
Nothing for them to fear
Somewhere out there.

Jake Anthony (11)
St Thomas More Catholic College, Stoke-on-Trent

My Holiday

It's that time of the year
When everyone raises a cheer.
The school is finished for the break
And the family holiday is ready to take.
Mum and Dad have finished their work
And I have got no homework.
The cat is going to the cattery
To recharge her battery.
Bulgaria is the destination
Where we will get some relaxation.
Two weeks of fun in the sun
Then the holiday is done.
Then we say goodbye with a tear
But we will be back next year.

Daniel Kane (12)
St Thomas More Catholic College, Stoke-on-Trent

Fireworks

A rocket standing tall and proud,
When set off is sure to be loud;
Exploding high up into the sky,
With showers of sparkling white.

A Catherine wheel spinning round and round,
Making a hissing and whirling sound;
Spinning and twisting in the night,
Making sparkles nice and bright.

Roman Candles tall and thin,
So enjoyable they make you grin;
Sparkling and fizzing for a while,
They just make you smile.

A sparkler thin and held in the hand,
But does not produce a nasty bang;
Glittering and sparkling and burning away,
All this for one special day.

Ben Diliberto (11)
St Thomas More Catholic College, Stoke-on-Trent

Bonfire Night

Bang, bang, bang,
All night long.
There goes the clock,
Ding, dong, dang.

Fireworks,
Fireworks,
Oh so bright,
Fireworks,
Fireworks,
Light up the night!

Joelle Littlejohn (12)
St Thomas More Catholic College, Stoke-on-Trent

The Mysterious Figure

Can you hear the black crow cry
Or see his loose sleeve flap around
In the wind like a wild dog?

You hear a whistle,
You hear a caw
See a figure cry some more.
Fear comes upon you
As you hear an owl coo.

Think of a thought
So fearsome, so wrong
A feeling shivers down your spine
Like a cold you have caught.

Wanting to go more
Every single day
Because the sight in front of you
Was left to decay.

Kelly Bryan (11)
St Thomas More Catholic College, Stoke-on-Trent

A Friend

Side by side
Together we travel
This long journey
Never to be apart.

Together we stand
Like peas in a pod,
Through thick and thin,
Until our final seconds.

Jake Smith (11)
St Thomas More Catholic College, Stoke-on-Trent

In The Cave

In the cave,
There are lots of bats
And with them
Are giant rats.

In the cave,
Where no one goes,
There are things
That no one knows.

In the cave,
There are loads of monsters,
Go in if you dare,
You'll have a nightmare.

In the cave,
Where no one goes,
There is a thing
That no one knows.

Ryan Fulcher (11)
St Thomas More Catholic College, Stoke-on-Trent

Creepy Cauldron

Rats that squeak
Wolves that howl
Both of these
Are really quite foul.

Ghosts and ghouls
Eerie and white
Screaming is heard
When you're given a fright.

Owls that hoot
Dogs that bark
Both of these
Eat at dark.

Jonathan James Toft (11)
St Thomas More Catholic College, Stoke-on-Trent

My Dream

I dream of a place where nobody has been
A world created by the thoughts I send
A cry in the dark unheard
As the thoughts I dream begin to unfurl
Not all dreams begin with pleasure and fun
Not all my dreams begin with the rising of the sun
Some of my dreams become my worst fears
When in this realm of sorrows and tears
A scared little child we all become
When we're in the dark we start to cry
It goes unheard by others' eyes
We're proven wrong by the setting sun
For we know now another day will come
And that's true for all and not just some
So it begins the cycle repeating
But that won't stop my infinite dreaming.

Ruby Davies (11)
St Thomas More Catholic College, Stoke-on-Trent

The Dentist

The building was there a footstep away,
It was really happening and happening today,
There in front of me the big door,
My heartbeat too loud to ignore,
And there it was the dentist's chair,
My fear spread throughout the air,
In desperation I looked at the clock,
Then my eyes darted back to the lock,
The dentist turned and leered at me,
I wanted to plead and be set free,
But there I was under the dentist's light
Swallowed in darkness left to wallow in fright.

Nathalie Woolliscroft (11)
St Thomas More Catholic College, Stoke-on-Trent

My Broken Luv

You came along and completed my heart,
But as soon as you left it snapped back in half.
The tears were streams flowing down my pale cheeks,
The fear dark and gloomy like walking through a cave.
The loneliness shot through me,
I jumped as the pain struck fast
The thought of you not being here
None of it, nothing, feels right.

I no longer touch your soft pink cheeks
Or feel your breath on my forehead.
The world is spinning, and you, you're not there
To catch me as I fall.
I don't feel special anymore.
I can't feel your heart beat close to mine.
I'm falling deeper, deeper into a hole
But you're not there beside me
Holding me, making me feel
Like this is where I belong.

The phone hasn't rung once since you left,
I don't feel the tingling anymore when I receive a text.
I never imagined you'd leave me in this state,
Lying in the middle of a double bed without my other half.
I'm single, on my own now
You just had to ruin everything we had,
I can't understand what I did wrong
Why are you treating me so bad?

Your voice would make my heart smile,
Your touch made my teeth chatter.
Your eyes, they made the world lighter
Than it had ever been before.
I can't bear to see you with her,
The same way we used to be.
This new girl you've replaced me with
Do you even know who she is?

Why did you choose to do this?
Does it not hurt you to see me cry?
I mean, maybe it's me going crazy,
Maybe I need some help and therapy.
But if this is what 'luv' turns out to feel like
I'll try never to fall into it again.

Ashleigh Davies (12)
Sir Graham Balfour School

My Dog, Maisie

My dog Maisie,
Is just so crazy.
She is very small
But not very tall.

The colour of my dog is tan,
And I'm her biggest fan.
I love taking her for a walk
And trying to teach her to talk.

If we pick her up she grumbles,
She sounds like when my brother mumbles.
We sometimes call her Maisie Moo,
She amazes us what she can do.

She loves to play with other dogs
But does not like slimy frogs.
She also likes to play with our cat Dave,
It sometimes looks like they are having a rave.

She loves it when we give her food,
If she doesn't get any she is in a mood.
She likes to play with a ball
And runs to me when I call.

She hates it when we go in the car,
And she hopes we will not go very far.
Maisie Moo is the ideal pet,
The bestest friend I could ever get.

James Hewitt (12)
Sir Graham Balfour School

Bored

I've got no inspiration
And no anticipation
For this poem.
Thinking of a story,
All it does is bore me,
I'd much rather be
Somewhere else.
Thinking of my lunch,
I really want to munch
'Cause I'm really bored
In this class.
If only I was bright
I could see the light,
To tell me where
I'm going wrong.
Can't think of a verse,
It must be a curse.
There must be something wrong
With me today.
Still got no inspiration
Got no anticipation
For this poem.

Harry Farmer (12)
Sir Graham Balfour School

The End

Your sapphire eyes filled with tears
We both knew the end was near
Red liquid rolled down your arm
The silver glistening in your necklace charm.

We loved each other so much
Your soft hand was the last I touched
I loved you and I still do
Even Heaven is Hell without you.

Ellie Ralph (12)
Sir Graham Balfour School

Make A Stand!

Hey you!
Yer, you there
Standin' around
Like you just don't care.

Lookin' around
For somethin' to do
Trying to make a stand
For the small few.

People think you're all the same
Destroying things or
Lookin' for fame
But what do they know or care.

Now people are listening to you,
Everything that you say and do.
Maybe we might be able to
Change the world into something new.

Annabel Ryell (13)
Sir Graham Balfour School

Why?

'Why is the sky blue?
Why is blood red?
Why is water clear?
Why is it time to go to bed?

Why do we need a door?
Why do we need an elevator?
Why do we need sleep?
Why can't I go to bed later?

Why do dogs say *woof*?
Why do cats say *miaow*?
Why don't goldfish say anything?'
'Go to bed right now!'

Sam Paterson (12)
Sir Graham Balfour School

Life

Do we all move in predictable ways?
Do the pieces fit into place?
Are we spontaneous throughout our days
Or is this all a race?

Held captive in this world
Or is it a chance for life?
Step by step and don't be hurled,
No weapons! Put down that knife!

Have friends and have a family,
Love, care and teach them all.
Have fun and live happily,
It doesn't matter if you're small or tall.

You can choose your own path,
By happy, be sad.
Enjoy English, art or maths,
Be scared, be bad.

Enjoy yourself,
And don't be dull.
Be yourself,
Live life to the full!

Amy Howard (13)
Sir Graham Balfour School

Through The Window

Through the window I can see a beautiful garden.
Through the window I can see wild animals.
Through the window I can see a blanket of untouched
                    white snow, covering a wonderful village.
Through the window I can see a battlefield of soldiers
                              ready for the charge.
Through the window I can see an underwater party
                        with exotic fish and mermaids.
Through the window I can see, anything I want to see.

Daniella Richards (12)
Sir Graham Balfour School

The RWC

The Rugby World Cup is about to start
Sittin' wiv me dad the great old fart.
Wilkinson to Robinson he goes up
Falls to the floor and breaks his foot.
Will it all end
The English trend?
Will England be out?
What's all this about?
Jonny you're so slick
Just score this penalty kick.
Over the upright
But it was tight.
This is quite mean
As England lead 20-18.
The Aussies miss
Wat a bliss.
They're so lame
That could have won the game.
The whistle blows
And on they go.
And on we hack
To face the mighty All Blacks.

Andrew Peatfield (12)
Sir Graham Balfour School

What Can I Say?

Parents, parents, what can I say?
Do they really know what it's like today?
They live in a world so full of fear,
Always wanting to keep us near!

Kids, kids, what can I say?
Do they really know what it's like today?
With texts and games and MSN,
They want so much it never ends.

Amy-Rose Bayliffe
Sir Graham Balfour School

Midnight Stalker

My yellow eyes peer from a dark alleyway,
The wind whispers, the sky is grey.
My paws softly tread the ground,
I must be quiet, not a sound.
I hear scratching, I start to purr,
The moonlight dapples my jet-black fur.
My eyes start to dart,
I've mastered hunting to an art.

I crouch down low to the floor,
I slowly lift one mighty claw.
I see a long, thin, pink tail,
Curled next to the empty shell of a snail.
Then I strike, as quick as lightning,
For the mouse I assume this is rather frightening.
With one strike from my claw,
The poor little mouse is no more.

Suzanne Butters **(12)**
Sir Graham Balfour School

My Poetry

Don't tell me off,
'Cause I don't know how to stop,
Typing up this poetry,
Is really, really boring
So stop me now.
'Cause this is powerful stuff,
Run away while you can,
Before I will get to the end,
Then you will be doomed,
'Cause my poem wouldn't get you in the mood,
You would feel down,
'Cause I'm writing my doom poem.

Sam Alexander **(12)**
Sir Graham Balfour School

How, How, How

How, how, how can it be,
That those words won't come to me,
When I'm thinking and thinking of something to write,
It tends to bug me all day and night.

How, how, how can it be,
That those words won't come to me,
When I'm thinking and thinking of something to read,
It tends to remind me there's something I need.

How, how, how can it be
That those words won't come to me,
When I'm thinking and thinking of something to drink,
It tends to make me stop and think.

Hazel Jackson (12)
Sir Graham Balfour School

Claire

She is something,
Quiet,
Fun, clever,
It's not fair to be honest with you.
I like the way she talks to herself in maths,
She can speak my language,
She makes me laugh when I should be working,
She's crazy when she lets herself be,
When she doesn't understand a question her
Cheeky smile appears on her face,
I think I like Claire.
Yes, she's a great friend.

Olivia Graham (12)
Sir Graham Balfour School

Homeless

Do they know what it's like
to be alone?
Do they know how it feels
to have no home?
Do they know what it's like
to sleep in a box?
Do they know how it feels
to sit and beg?
Do they know how it feels
to have no shower?
Do they know what it's like
to have no food?
Do they know how it feels for
people to stare?
And do they even care?

Carissa Alderman (13)
Sir Graham Balfour School

Autumn Madness

Leaves are falling along the ground
Crunch, crunch under my feet
Hallowe'en is near
Orange pumpkins all around
It's that time of year
Have no fear
Strange creatures tend to appear
With this in mind
Autumn's here!

Macauley Blencowe (13)
Sir Graham Balfour School

Sad I Ams

What is it like to be other things,
I don't know . . . let's see

I am the empty paper cup
I am the doorbell
I am the light bulb
I am the letterbox.

I am fed up of being used
I am fed up of being pushed
I am fed up of being lit
But most of all I don't like being pushed
     by the postman . . .

Well . . . I'm glad I'm John.

John Handley (12)
Sir Graham Balfour School

A Man Called Bill

There once was a man called Bill,
Who lived on a great big hill,
He fell down it at great speed,
Into a bucket of animal feed,
And he remains in that bucket still.

Kyle Cooper (12)
Sir Graham Balfour School

The Poem For The World

The Earth is beautiful green and blue,
We must look after it me and you.
Get rid of the cars, keep all the trees,
Make sure you save electricity.
Let's all stand united, together we'll see
The world can live in harmony.
We are all equal, black and white;
It makes no difference, dark or light.
Don't walk by the people of the street,
Care for the people every day that you meet.
Love each other, don't judge by the face,
And together we'll make Earth a better place.

Helen Rogers (12)
Sir Graham Balfour School

Me And My Little Brother

I sit in my room by myself,
Listening to the music.
My little brother has to be near Mum.

I have my own laptop,
My little brother shares it,
Only when I say he can.

I go to college with my mates
And we do lessons in woodwork.
My little brother is still at school.

It's good being me.
It's good making choices.
I am glad I'm the older brother.

Lee Rudd (17)
Two Rivers Sixth Form

My Life

I love being me,
I love being cool, stylish and outgoing,
I love being funny,
A loyal person who loves having fun,
I am a chatterbox,
I am kind to people.

I love clothes,
I love being a healthy, cool guy like my family,
I have a happy loud family,
I love doing exercise and workouts,
I love pets, my family loves pets.

I love comedies,
I love chat shows,
I love DVDs,
I love music channels.

I love being young and fit,
I love being so cool and nice.
I love being sixteen years old.

Dan Berry (16)
Two Rivers Sixth Form

Motorbike Ride

I can ride a motorbike fast.
It's cool as I jump over rivers.
The engine roars,
The brakes squeal,
But in my head it's quiet as I think . . .
About the bike,
About the ride,
About being free.
It's fun being young,
Being in control of the bike,
Being in control of my life.

Shane Moore (16)
Two Rivers Sixth Form

When I'm Eighteen

When I'm eighteen
I can go to the pub,
I can drive,
I can leave home,
I can be independent,
Make my own decisions,
Rule my own life . . .
Because I will be an adult.

But for now . . .
I have to go to school,
I have to do as I'm told.
My mum chooses my clothes,
My mum decides my hairstyle,
She tells me I am wearing too much make-up
Because I am a child.

My generation is told what to do,
And when to do it,
And how to do it.
It's not fair.
I know what I want to wear,
What I want to do,
And how I want it done.
But I'm not allowed!

Ann-Marie Robbins (17)
Two Rivers Sixth Form

I Wish I Was Older

I wish I was older
I could go and see my boyfriend.
I could go shopping by myself.
I could wear make-up.
I could have my nails and hair done.
I could live by myself.

But if I was older
I'd have no teeth.
I'd forget things.
I'd get angry with my neighbours.
I'd be boring.
I'd wish I was younger.

It's good to be my generation,
I'm pretty,
I have lots of friends.
I have a laugh.
I can use an Xbox.
I like being me.

Claire Griffiths (17)
Two Rivers Sixth Form

It's Good To Be My Age

I can go out with my friends.
We go to town,
Go to the market,
Laughing, giggling, enjoying ourselves.
Hanging out with mates.

If I was younger
I couldn't go to town on my own
I'd have to stay with my mum
Everyone would be telling me what to do.

If I was older
I'd have to go to work every day,
I'd be too tired to enjoy myself.
I wouldn't understand computers.

It's good to be my age.

Nicole Sayce (16)
Two Rivers Sixth Form

Young Writers Information

We hope you have enjoyed reading this book - and that you will continue to enjoy it in the coming years.

If you like reading and writing poetry drop us a line, or give us a call, and we'll send you a free information pack.

Alternatively if you would like to order further copies of this book or any of our other titles, then please give us a call or log onto our website at www.youngwriters.co.uk

Young Writers Information
Remus House
Coltsfoot Drive
Peterborough
PE2 9JX

(01733) 890066